THE FOURTH QUARTER

embracing what matters most

OF YOUR LIFE

ALLEN HUNT &
MATTHEW KELLY

wellspring

ISBN: 978-1-63582-267-0

Designed by Ashley Dias

10 9 8 7 6 5 4 3 2 1

FIRST EDITION

Printed in the United States of America

The afternoon knows what the morning never suspected.

ROBERT FROST

"Don't just love,
astonish people with your love.
Don't just dabble in generosity,
live a life of
staggering generosity."

For Franca Oreffice and James Rafferty.
With thanksgiving for your love and generosity!

Table of Contents

Introduction:
Are You in the Fourth Quarter of Life?

"What lies behind us and what lies ahead of us are tiny matters compared to what lies within us." — Henry David Thoreau

What makes aging unbearable is the mistaken belief that it can be avoided. It cannot. You know that. We know that. But still, we persist in our avoidance and denial. Our efforts to avoid the unavoidable make us miserable.

Whether you are in the fourth quarter of life or not, this book will change the way you see yourself and the rest of your life. It is never too early to think seriously about what matters most. Many readers will wish they had been exposed to these ideas earlier in life, even those who are not yet in their fourth quarter.

If you find yourself in that state of mind, I encourage you to consider two ideas. First, you are reading this at exactly the right time for you. Second, make it part of your fourth quarter mission to share it with younger people.

Are you in your fourth quarter of life? Let's take an honest look.

A sixty-five-year-old man told me last week that he was still in his first quarter. Was he joking? Yes. But in the joke was an underlying inability to face the reality.

I read an article by a famous journalist recently who explained that at fifty-nine he was entering the second half of life. I was confused by his math. He went on to explain that he did not count the first eighteen years of his life in his calculation.

Our inability to be honest with ourselves about whether or not we are in the fourth quarter is itself a sign that we are unprepared for this stage of life.

We deceive ourselves in so many ways throughout life. It is time to root out those deceptions. It's time to be brutally honest with yourself. The older you get the more profoundly this honesty will serve you.

The first lie surrounds where we are in the life cycle. Lots of people talk about the first half of life and the second half of life. At what age does the second half start?

When we speak to people about the fourth quarter, most people think in terms of 100 years and divide it by four. But only one percent of people live to 100 years old. The average life-expectancy of an American is about eighty. Thirty-five percent live to ninety.

How would you feel about a football coach who told his players there were twenty-five minutes left in the game when there were actually only five minutes left?

WHAT QUARTER ARE YOU IN?

- If your age is between 1 and 20, you are in the first quarter.
- If your age is between 21 and 40, you are in the second quarter.
- If your age is between 41 and 60, you are in the third quarter.
- If your age is between 61 and 80, you are in the fourth quarter.
- And, if you are older than 80, you are in BONUS TIME!

Take a clear-eyed look at where you are in the cycle. This is a time to get brutally honest with yourself in every way. This honesty will serve you powerfully in the fourth quarter.

Self-deception, avoidance, and denial lead to fourth quarter fumbles that can make the whole difference.

TWO OF THE BIGGEST FOURTH QUARTER FUMBLES ARE:

1. Denying natural limitations.
2. Pretending that our self-made faults are natural limitations.

The questions and exercises in this book will help you thrive in the fourth quarter. Some of the questions will fill you with great hope and joy. Others will challenge you to face uncomfortable truths. Both have a role to play.

Our hope is to raise awareness about the unique opportunities and obstacles the fourth quarter of life presents and provide you with a practical guide to help you discern all you encounter during this season.

THE PURPOSE OF THIS PRACTICAL GUIDE IS TO HELP YOU...

- Live the fourth quarter based on proven life principles
- Clearly establish meaning and direction for your life
- Develop the clarity necessary to make good decisions
- Identify your hopes and dreams
- Establish what you need and want most at this time in your life
- Learn to say no

There are many ways to use this book. You can work your way through from start to finish. You can jump around. You could go away on retreat or pilgrimage and work through the whole book. You could do one chapter a day, but there is no rush, and some chapters may require a whole week of reflection. There may be single ideas that call you to linger and reflect. Allow the Spirit to guide you.

If you skip an exercise or a whole topic, that's okay, but think about why. Are you avoiding something? Not ready for something? Resisting something? And what are the feelings that go along with whatever you are skipping? Is there pain there? Fear? Unrealized hopes and dreams? There may be good reasons for each of these responses, but it helps to be aware of what is happening within you.

Intentionality is the key to successful fourth quarter living. People don't accidentally age gracefully. People don't accidentally die peacefully. And people don't accidentally leave behind legacies of hope, love, and encouragement.

All these things require intentionality. The questions and exercises ahead will help you develop that intentionality.

Football games are won or lost in the fourth quarter. We have all seen it. It can be heartbreaking or exhilarating. But football is just a game. Life isn't. There is a lot more at stake.

What's at stake? Everything.

It is time to sift the vital few from the trivial many. It is time to discern what matters most. It is time to dedicate ourselves to what is essential.

Whether you are sixteen or sixty,
the rest of your life is ahead of you.
You cannot change
one moment of your past,
but you can change your whole future.
Now is your time.

THE RHYTHM OF LIFE

1.

The Unavoidable Truth

You are going to die. This is the unavoidable truth. Life is a death sentence. From the moment we are born we are dying. This may sound morbid, still it is true. And the fourth quarter is no time to deal in half-truths.

"Remember, you are dust and unto dust you shall return," the Scriptures remind us in Genesis 3:19. God wants us to remember this truth because being mindful of this reality leads us to live life more fully. The reality of death puts the majesty of life into perspective.

The shortness of life allows us to see that most things in this life are trivial and only a few things really matter.

How long will you live? We ran through some life expectancy averages in the introduction. They are helpful because they drive intentionality. It's helpful to have a sense of where you are in the journey. But nobody is promised tomorrow.

HOW LONG DO YOU HAVE LEFT? The greatest predictor for most people is the age their parents passed. How old were your parents when they died? If your parents are still living, how old are they? How old were your grandparents when they died?

FATHER

PATERNAL GRANDFATHER

MATERNAL GRANDFATHER

MOTHER

PATERNAL GRANDMOTHER

MATERNAL GRANDMOTHER

There is something about approaching the age at which our parents passed. It sends people deep into reflection. I have seen men and women completely unravel at this time in their lives, primarily because they didn't realize what was happening until later, and they didn't make time to reflect on what was stirring in their souls. Make time for prayer and reflection as this time approaches for you.

Is death the bottom line? No. That's why people think talk of death is morbid, because they think it is the bottom line.

The truth is we are pilgrims. We are just passing through this place. Heaven is our true calling.

When my son Ralph was five-years old, he came into my study one night before bed. I gave him a huge hug and kiss, and I said to him: "Goodnight my beautiful boy. You are just delicious. I love you for two forevers!"

"No Daddy!" He replied.

"What do you mean?" I asked.

"There is only one forever!"

"Really?" I asked.

"Yep. This life is not forever! We are just passing through this life. The only forever is in Heaven."

Powerful! From the mouths of babes. This life is not forever! We are just passing through this life. Take one minute each day to meditate on this truth. The reality of death rearranges our priorities.

Death comes to us all. One day you will make the journey from this world to the next. Nobody knows when, but everybody knows it will happen. It is unavoidable. When death approaches, the person you have become meets the person you could have been. This is a humbling encounter. Don't wait for it. Meet with the person you are capable of becoming for a few minutes each day. The more time you spend in these meetings, the less you will fear death. Use your thoughts, words, choices, and actions, to close the gap between who you are today and who you are capable of being. This is the path that leads to a deeply fulfilling fourth quarter.

The shortness of life is an invitation to grasp every moment and experience it fully.

Give people the benefit of the doubt.
Life is difficult and messy,
and everyone is carrying a heavy burden.

LIFE IS MESSY

2.

The Liars and Charlatans

Even though death is unavoidable. Even though there is a 100% mortality rate in your city (and mine). There are still plenty of people living as if they were going to live forever, and plenty of people who will gladly foster that delusion in you if you let them.

Would you believe someone who told you he could turn back time? Or someone who told you she could hold back the tide? Or someone who told you he could make time stand still?

It may all sound foolish, but marketing companies deceive people by leading them to believe this foolishness in new ways every day.

Our culture is obsessed with the myth of staying young. It makes sense. Modern popular culture is an atheist. And not only does it not believe there is a God, but it also doesn't believe human beings have souls. From that mistaken perspective, it makes sense to obsess about youth and the body.

But for those of us who believe that God exists and that human beings have eternal souls, the second half of life, and the fourth quarter in particular, are about letting go of the cultures delusions and embracing God's vision for this life and the next.

Don't get caught up in the quest for eternal youth. Don't allow the liars and charlatans to lure you away from fully experiencing this season of life. Don't allow yourself to be deceived, and don't deceive yourself.

"60 is the new 50," they were saying a few years ago. Then they started saying, "70 is the new 50." And just last week I saw a segment on television talking about "70 is the new 40."

Trying to relive the third quarter when you are in the fourth quarter is a significant error. Trying to relive your college experience during mid-life is a mistake. Seasons have reasons. Each stage of life has a purpose.

Things which matter most must never be at the mercy of things which matter least.

GOETHE

IDENTIFY THREE WAYS YOU HAVE ATTEMPTED TO STAY YOUNG, PRETEND YOU WERE YOUNGER, OR REJECT THE REALITY THAT YOU ARE IN THE FOURTH QUARTER OF LIFE.

....

....

....

The lines on your face tell the story of a lifetime of smiles and the heartaches and sacrifices you have endured to love and learn.

Let the young have their physical beauty. Elevate your pursuits to wisdom and soul beauty. Fill your days with wisdom, live that wisdom by aging gracefully, share that wisdom with the people who cross your path, and the beauty of your soul will shine for all to see.

3.

Five Signs of a Successful Fourth Quarter

What's needed for a successful fourth quarter? The answer to this question is different for every person in some ways, but these five signs are universal markers: Physically Active Lifestyle; Mental Stimulation; Social Engagement; Meaning and Purpose; and Spiritual Vitality.

GIVE YOURSELF A SCORE BETWEEN 1 AND 10 FOR EACH MARKER. AT 10 YOU ARE THRIVING, AT 5 YOU ARE SURVIVING, AND AT 1 YOU ARE HURTING.

PHYSICALLY ACTIVE LIFESTYLE

1 · 2 · 3 · 4 · 5 · 6 · 7 · 8 · 9 · 10

MENTAL STIMULATION

1 · 2 · 3 · 4 · 5 · 6 · 7 · 8 · 9 · 10

SOCIAL ENGAGEMENT

1 · 2 · 3 · 4 · 5 · 6 · 7 · 8 · 9 · 10

MEANING AND PURPOSE

1 · 2 · 3 · 4 · 5 · 6 · 7 · 8 · 9 · 10

SPIRITUAL VITALITY

1 · 2 · 3 · 4 · 5 · 6 · 7 · 8 · 9 · 10

What did you base your scores on? Your current abilities or the peak times in your life for each of these five signs? For example, a physically active lifestyle might once have meant running three miles a day, and today it might mean walking to the mailbox.

If you didn't base your scores on reasonable current abilities, go back and redo the exercise. Don't erase your first scores, just set a line through them and circle your new scores.

Honest self-assessment is a critical life skill in the fourth quarter.

4.

The 12 Qualities of a Good Person

We live in a confused culture. We live in a time that proclaims good things are bad, and bad things are good, or that there is no such thing as good and bad. But your eternal soul knows that good and bad have always been at odds in this world, and are often at odds in our own hearts. There is no need to allow the confusion of our times to blur the vision of our souls.

We have a natural desire to be good people. We have other desires too, no doubt. We also yearn for the people we love to be good people. We don't talk about it enough, but goodness is essential to a healthy sense of self and thriving relationships.

What is a good person? It's a beautiful question, and it has a beautiful answer. But before we get to that, let's consider the bigger question.

In our quest for wisdom, we should always seek the bigger questions. All too often we settle for lesser questions. For example, many people at some time in their lives ask the question: How do I become successful? The bigger question is: What is success? The bigger questions always allow us to answer our questions more wholistically.

Beyond the question at hand (What is a good person?) the bigger question is: What is a person? A person is an individual human being, a child of God, uniquely created by God, and of infinite value.

This is one of the biggest questions of all, because everything depends on the answer to this question. Our philosophy of life is drawn from, and can be traced back to, our answer to this single question. What is a human being? Our beliefs and opinions on every topic are formed by the answer to this question. It is the question that impacts our worldview more than any other. It is the question that leads us to God. It is the question that leads us to a true and complete understanding of who we are as individuals and who we are together.

Who are you? Even if you have been unclear your whole life, now, in your fourth quarter, it is critically important that you get clear about who you are.

You are a child of God. You are heir to His Kingdom. You are a unique being of infinite value.

Several years ago, when I was writing *Decision Point*, I had these posters made to hang in my children's rooms. This is the version that hangs in my daughter's room. The boys have a similar version.

Human beings are capable of astounding goodness. The reason is because God has loved us first and has placed His capacity for good within us.

Now that we have answered the question: What is a human being? We can turn our attention to the question: What is a good person?

A good person strives to be honest, humble, generous, responsible, empathetic, selfless, patient, kind, moral, courageous, ethical, and grateful. These are the twelve qualities of a good person.

IS THE LIST COMPLETE? No. My father used to say, "You are in the presence of goodness when someone is happy for another person's success or good fortune."

ADD THREE QUALITIES OF A GOOD PERSON THAT YOU THINK ARE MISSING FROM THE LIST.

....

....

....

WHICH THREE OF THESE QUALITIES DO YOU MOST YEARN TO FOSTER AT THIS TIME IN YOUR LIFE?

....

....

....

Each of these questions and exercises, invites us to reflect deeply on the lives we have lived and the person we have become. Some people begin to drown in self-pity and shame as they begin to reflect on their lives. This causes most to abandon the reflection that is so critical to the fourth quarter of our lives. Abandoning this process because of things in your past is like refusing to go to the hospital when that is the only place your health can be restored.

You are not what has happened to you.
You are more than the worst thing you have ever done.
Every saint has a past and every sinner has a future.
Don't let your past rob you of your future.

Now is the time to flood your life with goodness. Flood your mind with goodness by reading books that elevate you. Flood your soul with goodness by developing the habit of prayer and other spiritual practices. Flood your relationships with goodness by embracing the twelve qualities above. And unleash a tidal wave of goodness in this world every chance you get by creating Holy Moments.

The good we do never dies! It lives on forever—in other people, in other places, and in other times. Let goodness be your legacy.

People say, "He is so smart" or "She is brilliant." People say, "She is so successful" or "He has achieved great things." But let this be said about you, "He is a good man" or "She is a good woman."

I AM THE *daughter* OF A GREAT **KING.**

He is my father AND MY GOD.

THE WORLD MAY PRAISE ME OR CRITICIZE ME.

IT MATTERS NOT.

HE IS WITH ME, *always at my side,* GUIDING AND PROTECTING ME.

I DO NOT FEAR *because* **I AM HIS.**

5.

The Rest of Your Life

When we are children, people ask us, what do you want to do when you grow up? When we are teens, people ask us, what do you want to study when you go to college? When we are getting ready to graduate, people ask us, what do you plan to do now?

These are just some examples, but some form of these questions are always being presented to us by others, by the culture, and even by our own inner dialogue.

What are you going to do with the rest of your life?

Unfortunately, in the current culture, these questions focus on "what" and "do." We pause too rarely to consider who we are becoming.

You see, all the doing only has value to the extent that it helps us become more fully who God created us to be. This is one of life's most important lessons, and one that most people never learn.

We are not here to do. We are here to be and become. So, what should you *do* with the rest of your life?

Only those things that help you become. Beyond that, we think that the answer to this question is always changing. It isn't. The answer to this question is the same at every time in our lives. And it is the same for every person.

Holy Moments. This is the answer to the question about what to do with the rest of your life. Whether you are 12 or 112 you should spend the rest of your life collaborating with God to create Holy Moments.

What is a Holy Moment?

"A Holy Moment is a single moment in which you open yourself to God. You make yourself available to Him. You set aside personal preference and self-interest, and for one moment you do what you prayerfully believe God is calling you to do."

The world is a bit of a mess. How did it get that way? Unholy moments. How can we make the world a better place for our children and grandchildren? Holy Moments.

You know everything you need to know right now to fill the rest of your life with Holy Moments. If you want to change your life, fill your life with Holy Moments. If you want to revitalize a relationship, fill it with Holy Moments. And the only way to change the world, a world we all know is desperately in need of change, is to fill it with Holy Moments.

One moment at a time.

Some moments are holy, some moments are unholy, and you get to decide. You can influence the outcome of most moments in your life. When we collaborate with God, we create Holy Moments. When we collude with our selfishness, we create unholy moments. We have all participated in both. We have seen the marvelous effects of Holy Moments and the devastating effects of unholy moments.

LIST FIVE HOLY MOMENTS THAT HAVE HAD A LASTING IMPACT ON YOUR LIFE.

....

....

....

....

....

Now, let me ask you: What are you going to do with the rest of your life? More of the same? Continue to distract yourself with meaningless nonsense? Focus on what you can get? Keep dreaming about a change you know you will never make? Or are you finally, once and for all, ready to do something about the nagging dissatisfaction in your soul?

The fourth quarter of life is a series of moments. They can be Holy Moments or unholy moments. You get to decide. You can collaborate with God or try to go it on your own. The choice is yours.

It only takes a handful of Holy Moments to flood your soul with joy. It only takes a handful of Holy Moments to discover a new and exciting vision of the rest of your life.

FIll your fourth quarter with Holy Moments. Nothing else will fill you with such unquenchable satisfaction.

Visit
HolyMomentsBook.com
for a FREE copy of
Holy Moments: A Handbook for the Rest of Your Life

6.

Do Not Be Afraid

Fear is central to the human experience and one of the most dominant emotions in our society today. We are afraid of losing the things we worked hard to buy, we are afraid of rejection and failure, we are afraid of certain parts of town, afraid of criticism, and afraid of change.

With aging comes new fears. Fear of death, maybe. But so many other fears can enter our hearts at this stage of life.

WHAT DO YOU FEAR?

- Running out of money
- Losing your independence
- Not being able to do the things you enjoy
- Not being able to engage with the people you love
- Leaving a mess
- Uncertainty of death

- Physical vulnerability
- Suffering
- Body breaking down
- Losing control of your faculties
- Mental deterioration

WHAT ELSE? NAME YOUR FEARS. THEIR POWER OVER YOU BEGINS TO DIMINISH WHEN YOU NAME THEM.

....

....

....

....

....

The most common phrase to appear in the Bible is "Do not be afraid!" In both the Old and New Testaments, this single phrase appears repeatedly. Throughout history God has been inviting us to set our fears aside and trust in Him.

Do not be afraid. This is one of the persistent themes in God's message to humanity. So, why do we have the capacity for fear? To keep us safe. To guide us along the path of life. To deter us from the path of destruction.

It's true that we should listen to God's invitation to set our fears aside and trust in Him. But there are some built in assumptions here. God's message isn't "Do not be afraid and do whatever you want." There are some very real reasons and valid situations in which we should be afraid.

It's probably healthy to have a little fear about neglecting what matters most in the fourth quarter. It is wisdom to fear separation from God.

Our courage comes from God when our hearts, minds, and souls are fixed on what is good, true, just, right, noble, and beautiful.

You are as young as your faith,
as old as your doubt,
as young as your self-confidence,
as old as your fear,
as young as your hope, as old as your despair.

DOUGLAS MACARTHUR

7.

What Matters Most?

What matters most?

How has that changed throughout your life?

Are you able to map out in your mind (or on paper) the times in your life when your priorities and values shifted for better or for worse?

What were the consequences?

What was won and what was lost?

Was it worth it?

What wisdom has all this placed in your heart that could be very valuable to other people in your life?

It is critically important in the fourth quarter to be clear about what matters most for you. The danger, if we are not clear about our priorities, is that we will continue to be mesmerized by trivialities and seduced by distractions.

"Things which matter most must never be at the mercy of things which matter least," was Goethe's counsel. It is true for any project, organization, or relationship, and it is especially true for life in the fourth quarter. And yet, every day, most of us prioritize things that matter least over the most important things.

WHAT MATTERS MOST TO YOU AT THIS STAGE OF LIFE? WHAT ARE YOUR PRIORITIES FOR YOUR FOURTH QUARTER?

Do your priorities align with your stated values? How can you tell? There are two clear, objective indicators to examine. Time and money. We spend our time and money on who and what we value the most. We may say our priorities are A, B, and C, but if we spend the majority of our time and money on X, Y, and Z, then it is clear that our life is out of alignment with our stated priorities.

Pretend you are an investigator trying to prove to a jury that your priorities and values are what you say they are. The investigator only has two pieces of evidence to use: your financial papers (checkbook, bank statements, and credit card statements), and your calendar or schedule. Could an investigator prove to a jury of your peers that your priorities and values are what you claim they are?

Row, row, row your boat
Gently down the stream
Merrily, merrily, merrily, merrily
Life is but a dream.

NURSERY RHYME

8.

Mistakes and Regrets

We all make mistakes. We make poor decisions for any number of reasons. Sometimes because we don't know what we don't know, and sometimes because of selfishness. These mistakes can lead to regrets.

What is a regret? A feeling of sadness, repentance, or disappointment over something you did or didn't do in the past.

Regrets are born when we ignore the voice of conscience that tries always to steer us along the best path. Regrets are born when we allow ego and selfishness to rule our hearts. Regrets are the result of neglecting what matters most.

Anyone who is honest, humble, and loving will have regrets. The question is, what do we do with them?

We live in an unapologetic and unforgiving culture. The culture tells you not to regret anything. But it doesn't matter how many times you tell someone not to have regrets, in the quiet moments of their lives, the regrets of their hearts will still stir. So, telling people not to regret anything doesn't help them deal with the real regrets of their lives in ways that are healthy and healing.

Decorated military veteran Steve Maraboli writes, "We all make mistakes, have struggles, and even regret things in our past. But you are not your mistakes, you are not your struggles, and you are here NOW with the power to shape your day and your future."

That future includes eternity. And you have the power not only to shape your future, but also to influence other people's futures. How you handle your regrets can lead to healing and forgiveness, or resentment and multi-generational wounds. It's up to you.

A man is not old
until regrets
take the place of dreams.

JOHN BARRYMORE

WHAT ARE YOUR REGRETS?

....

....

....

....

....

A few years ago, I was doing some consulting work at a large hospital. The hospital was implementing *The Dream Manager Program* for its nurses. The program helps people identify why they do what they do, what is important to them, and what their hopes and dreams are for the future. It has been incredibly successful in hundreds of companies, because sadly, most people have never been asked, "What are your dreams?" and most people spend more time planning their annual vacation than they spend planning their lives.

During the project, I spent quite a bit of time with a group of hospice nurses. I remember wondering over and over again, "How do they do it?" One day at lunch, I was sitting with five or six of them, and I asked, "When people are dying, what do they talk about?" They told me that people who are dying talk to the nurses about how they wish they had lived their lives differently. Here is a sampling of what those nurses shared with me, twenty-four things dying people wished they had done differently.

- I wish I'd had the courage to just be myself.
- I wish I had spent more time with the people I love.
- I wish I had made spirituality more of a priority.
- I wish I hadn't spent so much time working.
- I wish I had discovered my purpose earlier.
- I wish I had learned to express my feelings more.
- I wish I hadn't spent so much time worrying about things that never happened.
- I wish I had taken more risks.
- I wish I had cared less about what other people thought.
- I wish I had realized earlier that happiness is a choice.
- I wish I had loved more.
- I wish I had taken better care of myself.

- I wish I had been a better spouse.
- I wish I had paid less attention to other people's expectations.
- I wish I had quit my job and found something I really enjoyed doing.
- I wish I had stayed in touch with old friends.
- I wish I had spoken my mind more.
- I wish I hadn't spent so much time chasing the wrong things.
- I wish I'd had more children.
- I wish I had touched more lives.
- I wish I had thought about life's big question earlier.
- I wish I had traveled more.
- I wish I had lived more in the moment.
- I wish I had pursued more of my dreams.

These are the regrets of dying people, people who were out of time. Each regret contains a powerful lesson for those of us who are still living, an invitation to make the most of the time we have left.

We may all accumulate regrets as we journey through life. But there are ways to make amends and to make peace. It is possible to die without regrets.

9.

It's Time to Find Your No

Staying open to life in the fourth quarter is important, and we will talk more about that, but if you haven't found your no yet, it's time.

Most of us struggle to set healthy boundaries, especially in relationships that are unhealthy. The fourth quarter is a time to get clear about healthy boundaries in all of our relationships. And to do that you need to find your no.

When our children were very young, we taught them, as most parents do, how to politely decline if someone offered them something they didn't want.

"No, thank you," is the phrase we taught them.

It's simple. It's clear. And yet, it is amazing how difficult we find it to politely say that we don't want something as adults. Our minds get clouded by so many other ideas and considerations. What will people think? Maybe she won't like me if I decline the invitation? Perhaps I will never get invited again? On and on goes the normal and neurotic list of things we consider in saying yes or no to something.

Sadly, most of our considerations are trivial compared to what matters most. Is God calling me to say yes or no? Will this help me become the-best-version-of-myself? Is this the best and highest use of my time, effort, attention, and energy?

When my son Ralph was very young, he took to the phrase quickly, and weaponized it in very cheeky and love-able ways.

"It's time for your bath, Ralphie!" we would say. "No, thank you, Daddy!" he would reply.

"It's time for dinner, Ralphie!" his mother would say. "No, thank you, Mom!" he would reply.

"It's time to come inside now, Ralphie!" we would say. "No, thank you!" he would reply.

Now is the time to find your no. It is time to get very comfortable saying "No, thank you!" Is it easy? Only if you are in the habit of saying it. But the clearer you become about what matters most, the easier it becomes to say no to everything else. The best way to say no is to have a deeper yes. One of the very concrete goals of this book is to help you get clear about what your deepest yesses are, so that you can honor and celebrate them.

It also helps to keep in mind that when we say yes to what is not intended for us, we miss out on what God created just for us.

MAKE A LIST OF THINGS YOU KNOW YOU SHOULD HAVE SAID NO TO THROUGHOUT YOUR LIFE.

One other thing to keep in mind when you say no is that for most people the difficult part is not saying no. The difficult part is explaining why they are declining. The easiest way to move beyond this hurdle is to avoid it unless absolutely necessary. Don't explain. In most cases you are not required to.

Get comfortable saying no. Get comfortable not offering an explanation. There is fantastic liberation in both.

LIST THREE TO FIVE THINGS YOU NEED TO START SAYING NO TO.

No is your friend when it comes to embracing simplicity. In fact, no is your friend when it comes to implementing most of the lessons the ideas on these pages are stirring within us. Most of us know we need to get better at saying no, so I am not going to wax lyrical on the subject. I will just say this one thing and invite you to reflect upon it: *If you are not free to say no, you aren't free to say yes.*

Work on being free to say no and your yes will be more focused, meaningful, and powerful than ever before. What you say yes to determines everything. And if you don't say no to the wrong things there will be no room in your life to say yes to the right things.

Exercise: Sit quietly and imagine yourself saying, "No, thank you" in various situations. Say it out loud now. Say it out loud again. Say it gently and peacefully. Get comfortable saying it.

We say we want to live more meaningful lives, but we keep saying yes to meaningless things. Start saying no to meaningless things and allow a life of meaning and fulfillment to emerge within and around you.

10.

Time Wasters and Soul Destroyers

Is life long or short? Most people believe life is short. Many believe that life rushes by. Some discover at the end of life, when it is too late, that they are finally ready to live life. But it's too late because they spent their whole lives avoiding life's most crucial questions.

Now is your time to consider life's most crucial questions.

Most people agree that life is too short to waste, and yet, most of us waste a fair bit of time. We waste time procrastinating, we waste time on frivolous and trivial pursuits, we waste time withdrawing from people we love, we waste time accumulating things we don't need, and we waste time in unforgiveness.

Now, in this fourth quarter of life, it's important to take a clear-eyed look at the time wasters and soul destroyers in your life. These may be people, activities, habits, or thought patterns. Whatever your time wasters and soul destroyers are, it is time to name them and claim them, so you can exit them from your life.

Intentionality is essential in the fourth quarter. It's amazing how you can sit down in front of the television and spend hours there before you recognize exactly what is happening. It's astoundingly easy to get lost in social media for an hour or two. We each have our own examples of things we do unintentionally. They just sort of happen. These time wasters are dangerous at any stage of life, but they take on new weight in the fourth quarter.

These time wasters can also be soul destroying, but there are other soul destroyers that can take up residence in our hearts, minds, and schedules. Here are some examples of soul destroyers.

Think of yourself as dead.
You have lived your life.
Now take what's left and live it properly.

MARCUS AURELIUS

NINE SOUL DESTROYERS

- Avoiding silence, solitude, and the encounter with God they naturally lead us into.
- Watching too much television.
- Obsessing over what other people think.
- Prioritizing money and things over people.
- Trying to control people and situations.
- Chasing accomplishments at the cost of relationships and spiritual growth.
- Gossip.
- Abusive relationships.
- Neglecting your spiritual routines and rituals.

NAME 3 TIME WASTERS YOU NEED TO BE MINDFUL OF...

....

....

....

NAME 3 SOUL DESTROYERS YOU NEED TO BE MINDFUL OF...

....

....

....

When it comes to time wasters and soul destroyers, we all need to play offense and defense. We play offense by acting intentionally; we play defense by staying watchful for times when we are susceptible to falling into these traps.

Life is too short to be wasted. When we were children, a summer seemed to last forever. Now the years zip past at an ever-increasing pace, despite our best efforts to slow down and fully experience the moment.

Are you spending the time you have left intentionally?

For the foolish, old age is winter.
For the wise, it is the season of the harvest.

ANONYMOUS

11.

The Way to Clarity

Clarity is essential in the fourth quarter. We live busy, noisy, and distracted lives. The fourth quarter is a chance to do less, learn to enjoy peace and quiet, and live with passionate intentionality.

Your eyesight may begin to fade in your fourth quarter, but your soul-vision should get clearer with every passing day.

Clarity emerges from silence. When a situation emerges that requires you to focus and make a decision, you naturally seek silence, asking the people around you to be quiet, so you can concentrate. You know instinctively that clarity emerges from silence.

Simplicity is also a friend of clarity. Simplicity can come in many forms. A day with no commitments is a form of simplicity that can clear the mind and focus our hearts.

Another way to simplify our lives is to declutter our

space. We spend our lives consuming and collecting things. Things are great when you need them. But when you don't, they can clutter your space, which believe it or not can clutter your heart, mind, and soul.

There are two categories of things worth hanging on to: the things that you need and the things that bring you great joy. Everything else we should pass along to someone who needs it more or will enjoy it more.

The things outside of these two categories weigh us down. We don't realize it because we have been gathering them for so long. But once you start to declutter your space, you will be surprised at the weight you feel lifting. Decluttering gives birth to a real liberation.

Declutter your space and clarity will emerge. Give things away, throw things away. When someone comes to visit, give them something they need or something that will bring them joy.

Stuff is not your friend in the fourth quarter. It's a distraction. It occupies space in your heart and mind. Things require time, attention, and care, which leaves less time for what really matters. You don't want to be giving time, attention, and care to material things in your fourth quarter. You want to be giving your time, attention, and care to the people you love and to the journey of the soul. You have a finite amount of these precious gifts.

EXERCISE: IF THIS GOES HOW I THINK IT WILL, CONSIDER COMMITTING TO REMOVING SOMETHING FROM YOUR SPACE UNTIL YOU ARE DOWN TO JUST THOSE TWO CATEGORIES:

1. Things you need
2. Things that bring you great joy

Simplifying is countercultural. Decluttering is countercultural. So is joy. For all that we have amassed, has it brought us more joy? I think not. It is time to try a new path. The path of simplicity. The path of less.

It may seem paradoxical that doing less and having less is the path to joy, but you will find out it is true for yourself very soon. This is just one of many fourth quarter paradoxes that we are going to explore together.

Start today by putting these two lists together.

LIST TEN THINGS YOU WANT TO GIVE AWAY TO A SPECIFIC PERSON...

LIST TEN THINGS YOU KNOW YOU SHOULD PROBABLY GET RID OF...

Less is more in the fourth quarter. Spiritually healthy people consume less. Spiritually healthy people need less stuff. If you feel drawn to start consuming more, pay attention to what is happening within you. What void are you trying to fill with things? Decluttering your life is an enormous victory. Once you have done it, beware the temptation to fall back into a pattern of consumption and accumulation.

The Five Keys to Living and Dying with No Regrets

1. Say Yes to God: God invites you onto a wonderful journey. When you say yes to God's invitation, you know where you're going.

2. Focus on a Fourth Quarter Virtue: Pursue one fourth quarter virtue God has specifically placed in you. Then watch it create blossoms in all areas of your life.

3. Give. It. Away: The more you give yourself away, the happier you'll be.

4. Forgive. Often: Bitter and resentful is no way to live. And it's definitely no way to die.

5. Be Open to Life: Your fourth quarter can be more of a birthing than a dying. Be open to what can be.

Excerpt from *No Regrets:*

A FABLE ABOUT LIVING YOUR 4TH QUARTER INTENTIONALLY

12.

The Classroom of Silence

The older I get, the more I enjoy going to church. When I was younger, I got caught up in being critical of everything that was mediocre about the experience. Now, I am just there to spend time with my God and His family, and I am learning, slowly, to let go of all the other things, and rest in His peace. This transformation was not achieved just by the passing of time, but also by the growing awareness of my own flaws, faults, and failures. Our humanity is reflected in the majesty and the mediocrity of our experience at church on Sunday.

The fourth quarter is a time to explore the spiritual life like never before. The blunt truth is this: If you don't pray now, you are never going to pray. If you don't develop or solidify the habit of daily prayer in the fourth quarter, you will be ill-prepared to meet your maker.

There will always be excuses to be made. But our hope

is that this season of your life will be one of amazing spiritual flourishing. Reflect on those words for a few moments: AMAZING SPIRITUAL FLOURISHING. What would that be like? Have you ever tasted that kind of flourishing? Do you yearn for that?

MAKE PRAYER AND SPIRITUALITY A PRIORITY IN YOUR FOURTH QUARTER.

- Develop the daily habit of prayer.
- Go on a pilgrimage.
- Read great spiritual books.
- Read the Bible.
- Learn to sit in God's presence and just be.
- Keep a spiritual journal.
- Go on a silent retreat.
- Study the history of the faith.
- Say YES to God.

Ever since I began speaking and writing I have been encouraging people to begin one habit above all others: Spend ten minutes each day in the classroom of silence with God.

It will change you. It will change your relationships. It will change your life. It will transform you from a tourist to a pilgrim.

What's the difference between a pilgrim and a tourist?

Tourists want everything to go exactly as they have planned and imagined. They rush around from one place to another making sure they cram everything in. They are constantly buying souvenirs and knickknacks, many of which they will look at when they get home and wonder, "What was I thinking?" They are more interested in taking photos of their experiences than experiencing deeply the people and places they are encountering. Tourists get upset if there are delays. They demand prompt attention and service to their every need and desire. They focus on themselves, often shoving past others to get where they want to go. Tourists go sightseeing. Tourists count the cost.

Pilgrims are very different. They look for signs. If a flight gets delayed or canceled, they ask, "What is God trying to say to me?" Pilgrims are not concerned with seeing and doing everything, just the things they feel called to see and do. They are not obsessed with shopping. They are aware of the needs of others. Pilgrims are in search of meaning. Pilgrims count their blessings.

The reality is we are all pilgrims. This planet we call earth is not our home; we are just passing through. We build homes and establish ourselves here on earth in ways that ignore that we are just here for a short time. It is a dangerous pastime to live as if you were never going to die, but consciously or subconsciously we all fall into this trap to various degrees.

We are only here on earth for the blink of an eye. This is not our home. That's why the happiness that God wants for us is very different from the momentary pleasures of this world. God created us for lasting happiness in a changing world and eternal happiness with him in Heaven. The happiness He wants for us in this life is a rare kind of happiness that is not dependent on situations or circumstances. It is easy to be happy when everything is going well. But Christian joy is possible regardless of situations or circumstances.

The fourth quarter is time to adopt the heart of a pilgrim. Pilgrims are men and women of prayer, constantly in conversation with God about what is happening around them and within them.

If you do not know how to pray, we will teach you. If your prayer life has grown stale, we will give you the tool you need to reinvigorate it. It is called *The Prayer Process*.

No matter where you are in your spiritual journey, it will lead you into a deeply personal conversation with your God. The process expands and contracts to meet each person where they are in the journey on any given day.

Pick a time to pray each day. Make this a non-negotiable aspect of your daily schedule.

If you feel called to explore
this topic more,
we invite you to read
I Heard God Laugh

Soul,
You have the heart of a lion,
strong and courageous.
Let nothing distract you,
let nobody discourage you
from your daily communion
with the one who created you.

I HEARD GOD LAUGH

The Prayer Process

1. GRATITUDE
Begin by thanking God in a personal dialogue for whatever you are most grateful for today.

2. AWARENESS
Revisit the times in the past twenty-four hours when you were and were not the-best-version-of-yourself. Talk to God about these situations and what you learned from them.

3. SIGNIFICANT MOMENTS
Identify something you experienced in the last twenty-four hours and explore what God might be trying to say to you through that event (or person).

4. PEACE
Ask God to forgive you for any wrong you have committed (against yourself, another person, or Him) and to fill you with a deep and abiding peace.

5. FREEDOM
Speak with God about how He is inviting you to change your life, so that you can experience the freedom to be the-best-version-of-yourself.

6. OTHERS
Lift up to God anyone you feel called to pray for today, asking God to bless and guide them.

7. PRAY THE OUR FATHER.

13.

Your Bigger Future

How do you feel about your future? If you don't feel great about it, you may not be looking far enough into the future. One of the biggest mistakes we can make in the fourth quarter is to stop dreaming.

"This dreaming business is not for me; dreaming is for young people!" This is a comment we have heard over and over again at our Bigger Future events, where we encourage individuals and church communities to dream together. But the fourth quarter is no time to stop dreaming.

"Everything great in history has been accomplished by people who believed that the future could be bigger and better than the past." I have said this to literally millions of people since I published *The Dream Manager*.

I have no doubt that your future is going to be bigger than your past. I believe that because I ultimately believe what we experience in the afterlife is enormous. But between now and then, the key to having a better future may be having a smaller future.

This is another one of life's fourth quarter paradoxes.

We are raised to believe that bigger and more and faster are always better. This is another example of the joy-sucking lies that our culture feeds us with unerring consistency. The truth is:

- Sometimes smaller is better.
- Sometimes less is better.
- Sometimes slower is better.

All three are practical conduits that deliver joy to the soul. Give them a try. Pay attention to how your mood and disposition change. Take note of the clarity that emerges in your heart and mind. And notice that you will start breathing deeply again.

When was the last time you intentionally took a deep breath? When we get stressed, we stop breathing deeply. Stress causes us to take short, shallow breaths instead of long, deep breaths. Some people spend decades in the stress of shallow breathing.

Breathing deeply is a fourth quarter habit worth practicing and celebrating.

But here's the thing, just because we are talking about getting rid of stuff, simplifying, decluttering our space and schedule, smaller, less, and slower, doesn't mean it is time to stop dreaming. The fourth quarter should be a time rich with dreams, but this is a time for different dreams.

When I ask young people to put together a Dream List, it is often filled with things they want to buy and accomplish. There is nothing wrong with that. There are reasons and seasons for everything under the sun.

But our dreams should evolve as we mature. This is when people's dream job changes from the one that pays the most to the one that is dripping with meaning. This is also when people shift from wanting things to seeking experiences.

Now, in the fourth quarter, it's time for another shift. Most people's fourth quarter dreams surround becoming, preparing, relationships, and legacy.

This exercise may take longer than most. You may need to come back to it a few times in the coming weeks to get it right for you. Keep listening to the gentle voice within you, keep listening to God, and adjust your answers as many times as you need until your list feels right.

WHAT ARE YOUR FOURTH QUARTER DREAMS?

Make a list of ten dreams you would like to experience in your fourth quarter and beyond. Don't judge your dreams, just write them down.

If you are not sure about some of the dreams you list after a few days or weeks of reflection, consider what is it that makes you uneasy about them. Ask yourself: Why do these particular dreams matter to me? Go through the list one by one and examine the motives in your heart behind each of these dreams. Our motives provide powerful insight into who we are and what we value.

The ability to dream is one of the most astounding gifts God has given us. It is one of the many things that makes human beings unique. We have the ability to look into the future, imagine something better, and then return to the present moment and act to bring about that better future.

You may be in the fourth quarter of life, but this is no time to stop dreaming. What are your dreams?

Your dreams are your dreams for a reason!
Do not say I am too old.
Do not say I am too young.
Now is your time.

THE DREAM MANAGER

14.

What's Your Story?

Knowing our personal story and sharing our personal story is part of every culture. How familiar are you with your own story? Have you forgotten important episodes and happenings from your journey? Have you been sharing your story with those closest to you?

The fourth quarter is a time to remember. The following questions are designed to help you remember your story. You are unlikely to sit your children and grandchildren down and tell them your entire story, but there are opportunities to share aspects of our stories in almost every encounter. Sharing our story helps others to see that life is full of ups and downs. This gives them hope in the face of their own difficulties, courage in the face of challenges, and gratitude for the blessings that fill their lives.

WHAT IS YOUR FULL NAME?

....

WHY DID YOUR PARENTS CHOOSE THIS NAME?

....

....

WHAT WAS YOUR PLACE AND DATE OF BIRTH?

....

WHAT HOSPITAL WERE YOU BORN IN?

....

WHAT HAS BEEN YOUR FAVORITE BIRTHDAY CELEBRATION
THROUGHOUT YOUR LIFE? WHY?

....

....

WHAT IS YOUR FAVORITE CHILDHOOD MEMORY?

....

....

....

....

WHAT SCHOOLS DID YOU ATTEND?

....

....

....

WHAT WAS YOUR ROOM LIKE GROWING UP?

....

....

WHAT WAS YOUR FAVORITE SONG AS A TEENAGER?

....

WHAT BOOKS HAVE INFLUENCED YOUR LIFE THE MOST?

....

....

....

WHAT'S YOUR FAVORITE MOVIE? WHY?

....

WHAT VIRTUE DO YOU MOST APPRECIATE IN YOUR FRIENDS?

....

....

....

WHAT IS YOUR BIGGEST FEAR?

....

DID YOU PLAY SPORTS?

....

WHERE DID YOU GO TO CHURCH AS A CHILD?

....

....

....

WHAT DO YOU REMEMBER ABOUT GOING TO CHURCH AS A CHILD?

....

....

....

DID A TEACHER, COACH, OR MENTOR HAVE GREAT IMPACT ON YOUR LIFE? WHO WAS THAT PERSON AND WHY WAS THEIR INFLUENCE SO GREAT?

....

....

....

WHEN YOU WERE A CHILD, WHAT DID YOU DREAM OF DOING WHEN YOU GREW UP?

....

....

....

WHAT WAS YOUR FIRST JOB?

....

....

AT WHAT TIME IN YOUR CAREER WERE YOU MOST FULFILLED AND WHY?

....

....

....

....

WHAT DO YOU REMEMBER ABOUT YOUR WEDDING? (if you are married)

....

....

....

....

WHAT ARE YOUR FAVORITE MEMORIES AS A PARENT? (if you have children)

....

....

....

....

....

HOW DID YOUR PARENTS INFLUENCE YOU (POSITIVELY AND NEGATIVELY)?

....

....

....

....

WHAT ARE YOUR BEST MEMORIES WITH YOUR SIBLINGS?
(if you have siblings)

....

....

....

DID YOU ENJOY TRAVELING?

....

....

WHAT TRIP OR VACATION PROVIDES THE FONDEST MEMORIES FOR YOU?

....

....

....

DO YOU STILL HAVE A VALID PASSPORT?

....

IS THERE SOMEWHERE YOU HAVE NOT BEEN THAT YOU ALWAYS WANTED TO GO TO?

....

....

WHAT DO YOU CONSIDER TO BE THE GREATEST ACCOMPLISHMENTS OF YOUR LIFE?

....

....

....

....

WHAT HAVE YOU LOVED ABOUT BEING A FATHER/MOTHER? (if you have children)

....

....

....

....

WHAT DO YOU LOVE ABOUT BEING A GRANDFATHER/GRANDMOTHER? (if you have grandchildren)

....

....

....

....

HOW HAVE YOUR CHILDREN EXCEEDED YOUR EXPECTATIONS?

....

....

....

....

WHAT ARE YOU MOST PROUD OF ABOUT YOUR CHILDREN?

....

....

....

....

WHAT DO YOU BELIEVE IS THE PURPOSE OF LIFE?

....

....

....

....

HOW HAVE YOUR SPIRITUALITY AND RELIGIOUS BELIEFS CHANGED OVER THE COURSE OF YOUR LIFE?

....

....

....

....

DO YOU BELIEVE IN MIRACLES?

WHAT ADVICE DO YOU HAVE FOR YOUR CHILDREN AND GRANDCHILDREN ABOUT LOVE?

HOW HAVE YOUR ATTITUDES TOWARD MONEY CHANGED
OVER THE COURSE OF YOUR LIFE?

....

....

....

NAME A LIVE PUBLIC EVENT THAT HAD A GREAT EMOTION-
AL IMPACT ON YOU (SPORT, MUSIC, POLITICAL, CHURCH,
SCHOOL, ETC.).

....

....

WHAT ONE BOOK WOULD YOU LIKE ALL YOUR CHILDREN
AND GRANDCHILDREN TO READ? WHY?

....

....

WHAT ARE YOUR HOPES AND DREAMS FOR YOUR CHILDREN AND GRANDCHILDREN?

WHAT IS SOMETHING ABOUT YOURSELF THAT MOST PEOPLE WHO KNOW YOU WOULD BE SURPRISED TO LEARN?

WHAT HAS BEEN THE BEST DAY OF YOUR LIFE SO FAR?

....

....

....

....

IF YOU COULD DESIGN A PERFECT DAY, HOW WOULD IT UNFOLD?

....

....

....

....

15.

Memories of the Past

I saw Barbara Streisand perform once. The feeling in the theatre when she sang the opening lines of *The Way We Were* was astounding.

> *Memories...*
> *Light the corners of my mind...*
> *Misty watercolor memories...*
> *Scattered pictures...*
> *Of the smiles we left behind...*
> *Smiles we gave to one another...*

I cannot think of that moment without a chill running up my spine.

Our memories are treasures. Big events and coincidences. Profound realizations and small awakenings of appreciation.

What are your favorite memories?

We have given you plenty of space here. Take your time. Go deep into your past and draw out as many memories as you can. You don't have to do it all in one sitting. Come back to the list over the coming days and weeks.

MY FAVORITE MEMORIES

Up to 12 years old...

During my teenage years...

....

....

....

....

In my twenties...

....

....

....

....

In my thirties...

....

....

....

....

In my forties...

....

....

....

....

In my fifties...

....

....

....

....

In my sixties...

....

....

....

....

The fourth quarter is a wonderful time to cherish memories of the past and a wonderful time to make new memories. Money and things are insignificant once our basic needs are attended to. It is memories and experiences that our hearts yearn for most.

Who do you most yearn to make memories with in this season of your life?

If you do everything
as if it were the last thing
you were doing in life,
and stop being aimless,
stop letting your emotions override
what your mind tells you,
stop being hypocritical, self-centered, irritable.
You see how few things
you have to do to live a satisfying
and reverent life?

MARCUS AURELIUS

10 PEOPLE I WOULD LIKE TO MAKE FOURTH QUARTER MEMORIES WITH

16.
Mapping Your Losses

Life is filled with great joys and deep suffering. We are given so much, but we lose so much also. It is easy to overlook our losses. But this often prevents us from healing. The fourth quarter is a unique time to look at the losses that are uniquely ours.

The exercise that follows is designed to help you identify, name, and claim the losses that have been part of your journey.

When we are experiencing intense loss, we don't necessarily register the loss. We focus on surviving. We minimize our loss. We say "I'm fine" when in truth we are hurting. We use all our effort and energy to move on. We may be afraid to explore our loss. We may fear we will never recover if we explore our losses.

Knowing what has been lost along the way, the price you have paid to become who you are today, is an important part of making peace with life in the fourth quarter.

What is your history of loss? Mapping your personal history of loss can be painful, but we think you will also find it deeply cathartic and spiritually healing.

Here is an example of one person's history of loss.

- Michael was born in 1954.
- 1959 (age 5). Michael's dog died. He didn't have any brothers and sisters and spent a lot of time with his dog. This loss had an oversized impact on him that he was not able to articulate at five-years-old to the adults around him. It was also a loss that the adults in his life minimized, setting in motion a life-long habit of minimizing his own losses.
- 1966 (age 12). Michael's family moved from Philadelphia to Los Angeles. Leaving all his friends behind was a traumatic experience that again was minimized by his parents.
- 1968 (age 14). Michael's cousin James was killed in the Vietnam War. James was the happiest person Michael had ever known, and the idea that he was dead at the age of nineteen seemed surreal.

- 1970 (age 16). Michael's first girlfriend broke up with him.
- 1974 (age 20). Michael's grandmother died. His grandmother had always been the person he felt most understood him. Her death left Michael feeling alone and adrift.
- 1979 (age 25). Michael's father died. He has mixed feelings about this, including significant guilt that he should have felt worse than he did about his father's death.
- 1987 (age 33). Michael's son died. Stricken by a rare blood disease his boy went from a happy, playful five-year-old to terminally ill in a matter of months.
- 1988 (age 34). Michael lost his job. Unable to process the death of his son he struggled to focus at work.
- 1991 (age 37). Michael's wife filed for divorce and was awarded full custody of their two living children.
- 2001 (age 47). Michael was diagnosed with cancer. He recovered successfully and is in full remission.
- 2007 (age 53). Michael's mother died.

We all have a history of pain and loss. It can be very helpful and healing to reflect on that history.

YOUR HISTORY OF LOSS

Take an inventory of the losses that have marked your life. Write down the year, your age at the time, and a brief description of the event.

Up to 12 years old...

....

....

....

During my teenage years...

....

....

....

In my twenties...

In my thirties...

In my forties...

In my fifties...

....

....

....

In my sixties...

....

....

....

In my seventies...

....

....

....

In my eighties...

....

....

....

At the end of life,
what really matters
is not what we bought, but what we built;
not what we got, but what we shared;
not our competence, but our character;
and not our success, but our signifiance.
Live a life that matters.
Life a life of love.

ANONYMOUS

17.

History of Celebration

Humanity has been marking time with celebrations for thousands of years. The Christian calendar is arranged around the major feast days of our faith. Secular calendars are arranged around both religious and secular holidays. Another way to look back on our lives in through the lens of celebration.

You don't stop laughing when you grow old, you grow old when you stop laughing.

GEORGE BERNARD SHAW

WHAT HAVE BEEN THE TEN MOST SIGNIFICANT CELEBRATIONS OF YOUR LIFE?

The one thing Christians do more than anything else is celebrate. Everything the Church does is centered around celebration.

We celebrate life. We celebrate the changing seasons with the richness of the Church's calendar. We celebrate excellence by honoring the saints and heroes of our faith. We celebrate birth and eternal life with baptism and burial. We celebrate truth, beauty, and goodness by seeking them out wherever they are to be found and honoring them in our everyday lives. We celebrate Christmas and Easter. We celebrate pilgrimage—our common journey and our individual journeys. We celebrate salvation. We celebrate forgiveness. We celebrate total dedication to the service of God's people with Holy Orders. We celebrate education. We celebrate communion with God and community with the Mass. We celebrate unity by seeking to bridge the gap. We celebrate love with marriage and children. We celebrate . . .

The spirit of Christianity is predominantly one of celebration, which is the genius and the fundamental orientation of our faith.

What do you celebrate? You have become the person you are today because of the things you have chosen to celebrate. Our culture has become what it is because of the things it celebrates.

You can celebrate anything you wish. You can celebrate life and faith. You can celebrate love and honesty, mercy and forgiveness, kindness and generosity. You can celebrate truth, beauty, goodness, and redemption. Or, on the other hand, you can celebrate destruction and paganism. You can celebrate hatred and violence, selfishness and greed, contempt and disrespect. You can celebrate perversion, corruption, pride, deceit, and condemnation. But one thing is certain: We become what we celebrate.

This is one of the immutable truths found in the life of every person who has ever lived. We become what we celebrate. It is true in the life of an individual, but also in the life of a family. It is true in the life of a nation, and it is true in the life of the Church.

Will your fourth quarter be a time of humble celebration or a time of stubborn resistance and mourning? We hope it will be a time of celebration.

WHO DO YOU WANT TO CELEBRATE IN THIS SEASON OF LIFE?

18.

The Unexpected

For all the planning we do, so much of life is unexpected. What have been the unexpected events of your life—positive and negative—and how did they impact you?

THE POSITIVE UNEXPECTED EVENTS OF MY LIFE...

....

....

....

....

....

THE NEGATIVE UNEXPECTED EVENTS OF MY LIFE...

....

....

....

....

....

The negative events of our lives can lead us to withdraw, isolate, and close our hearts. These responses are driven by fear and a desire to avoid similar pain and suffering in the future. Still, God invites us to stay open. Yes, staying open may expose us to the unexpected negative, but it also leaves us open to the astounding unexpected positive—and that is where we are most likely to find God in the fourth quarter. Not in all our plans, but in His one plan.

IN WHAT WAYS IS GOD INVITING YOU TO STAY OPEN TO THE UNEXPECTED IN THE FOURTH QUARTER OF YOUR LIFE?

....

....

....

....

....

If you want to make yourself and everyone around you miserable in your fourth quarter, try to control everything and everyone.

Stay open. The critical dispositions are to stay open to life, stay open to love, and stay open to God. Trust, surrender, believe, and receive. Stay open to the unexpected. Live in the hope that something wonderful is about to happen.

19.

Your 25-Year Plan

Do you have a plan for your future?

"Most people spend more time planning their annual vacation than they spend planning their lives." This is the one line from *The Dream Manager* that people bring up the most. It caught people's attention, because it is true, but also because it is a sad truth. The sadder truth is that most people have never been taught how to put together a life plan. Saddest of all is that most people have never been taught how to dream and plan with God. Well, today we are going to do something about that.

Now before we get too far, I want to set aside one myth about life-planning. The idea isn't to plan every moment. The idea is not to cling rigidly to the plan you come up with. The goal is to think intentionally about your future, so you can live intentionally in the present. The idea is to identify what matters most to you, and learn how to place what matters most at the center of your life.

This focus and intentionality will change your life forever.

The other option is to stumble along and just see what happens. We know this is a failing strategy. Napoleon said famously, "Those who fail to plan can plan to fail." It's time to come up with a life plan. A plan for the rest of your life...

Some people may say, "I am too old to put together a life plan." Nothing could be further from the truth. In fact, the older we get, the more important it is to reflect upon our future.

When people get close to the age of sixty, they tend to start thinking about the end of life. It is just something that happens. But the reality is, if you are anywhere in your fifties today and in reasonable health, you are likely to live for another 25 years . . . and not having a vision for those 25 years of your life would be a tragedy.

Everything great in history has been built by people who believed that the future could be better than the past. Do you believe that your future can be better than your past? Maybe you do, maybe you don't. Lots of people don't. All I ask is that you stay open to the possibility.

Stay open to a better future. It may not involve the same things as your past, it may involve new people, activities, and adventures.

Your better future may not be bigger than your past.

Bigger isn't always better. Sometimes a smaller, simpler future is a better future.

Only you know and that's why this visioning exercise is so important.

Many years ago, I met a master architect at a party. We got to talking and I asked her what area of architecture she worked in. She shared that her specialty was helping people design their dream homes, especially luxury custom homes.

"What is the biggest mistake people make when they are designing their dream home?" I asked.

She explained to me that most people make the same two mistakes. First, they do not make the areas around the kitchen large enough. This is the natural gathering space in a home. It is the place people gravitate toward when there is any type of gathering in a home.

Second, she explained, most people design the house they need today, and it takes between two and four years to design and build a luxury home. So, if you design the home you need today, by the time you move in, your needs have already changed, and depending on what stage of life you are in, those needs may have changed significantly.

"How do you help people avoid making these mistakes?" I asked next.

What I heard next was genius. She explained that she had her clients put together a 25-year plan. She explained that the focus of how most people use a home changes every five years, so by breaking the next 25 years into five-year increments, she helps her clients develop a vision for each five-year increment of the next 25 years.

The clients get a worksheet that is divided horizontally into five large areas. Down the left-hand column of the worksheet are blank lines for clients to list categories.

The first is age. How old are you today? How old will you be at the beginning of each of these five-year increments. If you are 55 today, you will be 80 at the end of the 25-year plan.

Next, she has her clients list their children and their ages in each segment of the 25-year plan. Then their grandchildren. Then their pets.

People quickly realize that their children will be grown and quickly off to college, and yet they may have been designing the home around their children.

She then has clients list every room in the home they are designing and describe how it will be used in each five-year-segment.

Ever since that night I have been using a similar process to help people form a vision for their lives. And today I encourage you to spend some time mapping out a vision for the next 25 years of your life. Over the next three pages you will find the worksheets necessary to complete this exercise.

Why 25 years if the fourth quarter for most people is about 20 years? There are a few reasons. We hope you live beyond the average life-expectancy and get some bonus time. It is important to visualize beyond the age at which most people die, otherwise our visualization could become a negative self-fulfilling prophecy. We hope many people will be introduced to this book long before their personal fourth quarter begins. And finally, we have been using this exercise for many years, long before we decided to write about the fourth quarter, it is known to many as the 25-Year Plan, and we do not want to create confusion by having a 20-Year Plan and a 25-Year Plan based on the same principle.

If I am older than sixty, should I do less than 25 years? No. The power of projecting far into the future is an important aspect of the exercise. Even if you are seventy when you do the exercise, do all 25 years. It will only impress on you even more the lessons the exercise is designed to deliver.

Across the top you will find the five columns, one for each five-year segment. Down the leftmost column you will find a number of categories.

We start with the same categories: Your age. Your spouse's name and age. The names and ages of your children. Names and ages of your pets.

Then you will find a whole bunch of categories. Jot down your vision for each of these aspects or areas of your life over the next 25 years.

Start with relationships. Identify a handful of relationships and describe how you would like to see them evolve over each time frame.

Then consider your home or living space.

If you own or lead a business, envision your business over the next 25 years.

Consider your career. How do you see it unfolding in each time segment and when do you envision it coming to a close?

Reflect on your health. What will be your health focus in each of the five-year increments?

Take a look at your personal finances. When do you hope to be debt free? Write it down. What do you plan to have saved by different ages? Jot it down. What do you plan to give away? To whom? And when? Put it in your plan. What other financial goals do you have over the next 25-years?

Next consider your mind. Your intellectual development and mental health. How do you plan to continue to feed and exercise your mind?

And then add other areas that are important to you. You may have a hobby that you want to continue to explore over the next 25 years. You may have new adventures you want to take as your commitments change over time.

25 years is over 9,000 days. Three months is just one percent of your next 25 years.

Most people overestimate what they can do in a day, and underestimate what they can do in a month. But most people never plan for a month. Most people overestimate what they can do in a year, but underestimate what they can do in a decade. And less than one percent of one percent of people even loosely plan out a decade of their lives in writing.

What can you do, be, and become over the next 25 years? Let's find out.

What are you going to focus on?

What area of your life could be improved tenfold? Yes,

ten times. Most of us have areas of our lives that can be massively improved if we have the right plan and the right coaching.

How would you like your life to be different five years from today? Do you have a plan? Most people don't. But today that is all changing for you.

There is a powerful line in Proverbs that reads, "Where there is no vision the people will perish." Do you have a vision or are you perishing? Starting today you are going to develop a vision for your life.

If you are interested in coaching
during the fourth quarter of your life,
visit
Q4Coaching.com
for more information.

There is nothing noble
in being superior to your fellow man;
true nobility
is being superior to your former self.

ERNEST HEMINGWAY

0-5 YEARS

Your Age	
Spouse's Name & Age	
Children's Names & Ages	
Pets' Ages	
Relationships	
Home/Living Space	
Business/Career	
Health	
Personal Finances/ Financial Goals	
Intellectual Development/ Mental Health	

6-10 YEARS

Your Age

Spouse's Name
& Age

Children's Names
& Ages

Pets' Ages

Relationships

Home/Living Space

Business/Career

Health

Personal Finances/
Financial Goals

Intellectual
Development/
Mental Health

11–15 YEARS

Your Age	
Spouse's Name & Age	
Children's Names & Ages	
Pets' Ages	
Relationships	
Home/Living Space	
Business/Career	
Health	
Personal Finances/ Financial Goals	
Intellectual Development/ Mental Health	

16-20 YEARS

Your Age

Spouse's Name
& Age

Children's Names
& Ages

Pets' Ages

Relationships

Home/Living Space

Business/Career

Health

Personal Finances/
Financial Goals

Intellectual
Development/
Mental Health

21-25 YEARS

Your Age	
Spouse's Name & Age	
Children's Names & Ages	
Pets' Ages	
Relationships	
Home/Living Space	
Business/Career	
Health	
Personal Finances/ Financial Goals	
Intellectual Development/ Mental Health	

If I find in myself a desire
which no experience in this world can satisfy,
the most probably explanation
is that I was made for another world.
If none of my earthly pleasures satisfy it,
that does not prove that the universe is a fraud.
Probably earthly pleasures were never
meant to satisfy it, but only to arouse it,
to suggest the real thing.
I must keep alive in myself the desire
for my true country, which I shall not find
till after death; I must never let it get snowed
under or turned aside;
I must make it the main object of life
to press on to that other country
and help others to do the same.

C.S. LEWIS

20.

What is God Saying to You?

Throughout the Bible we read about God communicating with people. God speaks! But for some reason we forget this, think He won't speak to us, pretend we didn't hear Him, and are afraid to really listen.

Learning to listen to God is one of the most exciting and daunting aspects of the spiritual life. Is it sometimes clear as day? Yes. Is it sometimes like deciphering code? Yes. Do we get it wrong sometimes? Yes. Is that part of the journey? Yes.

God is speaking to us all the time, the question is: Are we listening?

God is speaking to us all the time, but even when we do hear Him, we immediately begin to doubt—was that God or just thoughts in my mind?—all the time forgetting that sometimes God will use the very thoughts in your mind to communicate with you.

FOR THE NEXT 21 DAYS, WRITE DOWN THE ONE THING YOU SENSE GOD IS SAYING TO YOU.

Don't judge it. Just write it down. It may be the same thing serval days in a row, that's okay, write it down.

DAY 1 ....

....

DAY 2 ....

....

DAY 3 ....

....

DAY 4 ....

....

DAY 5 ....

....

DAY 6 ....

....

DAY 7 ....

....

DAY 8 ....

....

DAY 9 ....

....

DAY 10 ....

....

DAY 11 ....

....

DAY 12 ....

....

DAY 13 ....

....

DAY 14 ....

....

DAY 15 ....

....

DAY 16 ....

....

DAY 17 ....

....

DAY 18 ....

....

DAY 19 ....

....

DAY 20 ....

....

DAY 21 ....

....

21.
Living Meaningfully in a Trivial Culture

You cannot live a meaningful life by filling your life with meaningless things and activities. This is the fundamental truth we need to embrace if we are going to live more meaningful lives in the fourth quarter.

It isn't enough to stay busy, but busy can be deeply dissatisfying. The challenge is to fill your hours and days with meaningful things, activities, and encounters with people. This is a serious challenge in a world of unlimited opportunities.

We live in an age that celebrates triviality and builds pedestals for the most trivial. This bankrupt culture cannot help you navigate the fourth quarter. Living meaningfully in a trivial culture is no easy feat. It's time to step back, to step away, and forge a new path—a deeply meaningful path.

Where do we begin? Fill one hour with meaningful

interactions, activities, and things. It's amazing how you will feel the Spirit stirring within you after just one hour.

WRITE DOWN THREE ACTIVITIES YOU FIND MEANINGFUL.

....

....

....

WRITE DOWN THREE PEOPLE YOU CONSISTENTLY HAVE MEANINGFUL CONVERSATIONS WITH.

....

....

....

NAME THREE MATERIAL THINGS THAT BRING MEANING TO YOUR LIFE.

....

....

....

Somebody should tell us,
right at the start of our lives that we are dying.
Then we might live life to the limit,
every minute of every day.
Do it!
Whatever you want to do,
do it now!
There are only so many tomorrows.

POPE PAUL VI

22.

Your Fourth Quarter Virtue

Our lives only genuinely improve when we grow in virtue. The virtue of patience improves our lives. It improves our relationships. It improves society. Two patient people will always have a better relationship than two impatient people.

The same is true for generosity, perseverance, compassion, humility, and courage. Growing in virtue leads to both personal and spiritual expansion, which are the hallmarks of human flourishing.

DO YOU HAVE A FAVORITE VIRTUE? WRITE IT DOWN.

DO YOU HAVE A FAVORITE VIRTUE IN OTHER PEOPLE? WRITE IT DOWN.

....

Most people choose honesty. Without the trust that is born from the virtue of honesty, it's impossible to have a dynamic relationship of any type.

We cannot improve our lives in any meaningful way without improving as human beings. And what is true for one person is true for an entire society. Virtue is the only way for a society to make genuine progress.

Virtues are the building blocks of character. "Character is destiny," the Greek philosopher Heraclitus observed. This is true for a person, a marriage, a family, a community, a nation, and indeed, the whole human collective. Character is moral and ethical excellence; it is built one virtue upon another.

Virtue is at the heart of the fourth quarter. Everything important you will do in the fourth quarter requires virtue.

CHOOSE ONE VIRTUE TO FOCUS ON FOR YOUR FOURTH QUARTER. But don't just pick one. Pray about it. Ask God to guide you to the virtue that will guide and elevate this season of your life. This will be your fourth quarter virtue.

Why one virtue? Two reasons.

1. If you try to focus on many virtues, you will grow in none. Focus produces results.
2. All virtues are interconnected. You cannot grow in patience and not become more generous, courageous, loving, and kind. When you grow in one virtue, you grow in every virtue.

CHOOSE YOUR FOURTH QUARTER VIRTUE. Below is a list to choose from, but you are not limited by this list.

COURAGE

PRUDENCE

FAITH

HOPE

LOVE

JOY

PEACE

PATIENCE
KINDNESS
GENEROSITY
FAITHFULNESS
GENTLENESS
SELF-CONTROL
HUMILITY
JUSTICE

MY FOURTH QUARTER VIRTUE

....

The fourth quarter is a time to focus on character—and that means growing in virtue. If "Character is destiny" as Heraclitus suggests, you can predict the future if you know the virtue and character of a person, a couple, a family, a community, or a nation. When everything else is stripped away, and it all will be stripped away eventually, all that is left is character and virtue.

23.

Our Lives Change When Our Habits Change

Small habits can make a huge difference. Sometimes we compare our life today and the life we feel called to be living and we become overwhelmed. Sometimes we look at who we are and who we are capable of being and we become overwhelmed by the gap.

The sensation of feeling overwhelmed is a specific type of discouragement that doesn't come from God. God is the greatest source of encouragement in life. We may not always see that, but that is because of distortions in the way we see and experience God.

When we feel overwhelmed, it may be self-inflicted, it may be the result of unreasonable expectations other people have placed upon us, but it is not something God desires for us. And feeling overwhelmed is always proof that we are trying to do more than God is calling us to do, or trying to be something other than who God created us to be. His yoke is easy and His burden is light.

But regardless of all this, when we sense what is before us is insurmountable, when we become paralyzed by feelings of overwhelmedness, it's crucial that we remember that small changes can make a huge difference.

It's amazing how small habits can have outsized impact on our lives. Reading five pages a day of a great spiritual book, taking a walk each day, drinking plenty of water, are just three simple attainable examples.

What small new habits could have a huge impact on your fourth quarter?

There are habits that serve us powerfully at every stage of life. But each quarter invites us to establish a handful of new habits particular to that season of life. The fourth quarter also provides an opportunity to solidify habits that have always been important, but perhaps have never been given full priority in your life. These could include:

- The daily habit of prayer;
- Speaking your love;
- Intentional generosity;
- Reading books that feed your soul;

- Quality time with the people who matter most to you; and
- Physical exercise.

The fourth quarter is also an opportunity to develop habits that help you live into the final stages of life with grace and dignity.

WHAT THREE HABITS DO YOU FEEL CALLED TO DEVELOP IN YOUR FOURTH QUARTER?

....

....

....

24.

Your Content Diet

We live in a culture obsessed with physical appearance. One of the fruits of this obsession is the never-ending stream of diets that promise incredible results with effortless ease.

How would the world be different if we could see the state of our own soul? How would the world be different if we could see the state of each other's souls?

There is an optimal intake of food to fuel your body. We pay attention to our diet for the body on a daily basis. Not just the healthiest among us, but even those who have no desire to be optimally healthy spend time every day thinking about their diet, the choices they are making around food, and how that impacts their health and life. But are we paying attention to the diet of the mind and soul?

Many years ago, when I first began speaking and writing, I used to say to my audiences, "Give me a list of the books you are going to read over the next 12 months, and I will tell you how your life will change over the next year."

I believed then, and believe now, that we become the books we read. What we read today, walks and talks with us tomorrow.

The way we consume content has changed significantly over the past couple of decades, but I still believe that the content we consume has an enormous influence and impact on our lives. The content we consume impacts our lives because it influences our hearts, minds, bodies, and souls. It influences our decisions, and our choices sculpt so much of our lives.

Today I want to encourage you to take an inventory of the content you consume. As you do, consider the ways this content is impacting you positively and negatively.

How do you feel after consuming various content? Light, joyful, heavy, moody, happy, sad, anxious, depressed, hopeful, downcast, stressed, relaxed? Ask yourself: Does this content help make me a-better-version-of-myself?

Or, if you are bolder, and braver, it is worth asking yourself: Is this content helping me get to Heaven?

MY CONTENT DIET. Take an inventory of the content you consume on a regular basis. List the types of television shows you watch, newspapers and magazines you read, websites you visit regularly, music you listen to, conversations you participate in, and books you read.

....

....

....

....

....

....

....

The content we consume feeds the heart, mind, and soul. Some content encourages our hearts, other content is depressing and discouraging. Some content makes us better spouses, friends, parents, siblings, colleagues, and neighbors. But most content doesn't. Some content orients us toward God, other content leads us away from God.

It's time to get serious about your content diet.

25.

The Energy Factor

We face many limitations in life. Some of them real and some of them imagined. Time is a real limitation. Very often when people say they don't have time, what they really mean is they don't have the energy.

On average Americans spent 413 minutes each day on the internet last year. That's almost seven hours. Sure, some of that was for work or school, maybe even a bunch of it, but there is still a chunk that is non-essential. Is this what people most want to be doing with their leisure time? No. Why do they do it? Because they don't have the energy to do the things they most want to be doing.

On average Americans spend about three hours a day watching television. Is it what they want to be doing more than anything else in the world? No. But in many cases, they don't have the energy to do anything else.

Meanwhile, most people have hopes and dreams that they continue to put off. When asked the main reason why they have not pursued their hopes and dreams, the most common answer people give is, "I don't have time." In the vast majority of cases this isn't true. They have time, they just don't have the energy needed.

Our experience of life expands or contracts according to how much energy we have. That's no small thing. Think about that for a moment. Your experience of life is increased or limited by how much energy you have. We know this is true because we have all experienced a cold or the flu. What happens? We go into survival mode. We only do what is absolutely necessary. We rest and try to recover. But during that time that we are sick, our experience of life is limited, diminished, because we don't have the energy to do almost anything.

HOW IS YOUR ENERGY TODAY?

1 · 2 · 3 · 4 · 5 · 6 · 7 · 8 · 9 · 10

RATE YOUR ENERGY OVER THE PAST 12 MONTHS.

1 · 2 · 3 · 4 · 5 · 6 · 7 · 8 · 9 · 10

RATE YOUR ENERGY OVER THE PAST 5 YEARS.

1 · 2 · 3 · 4 · 5 · 6 · 7 · 8 · 9 · 10

WHAT WOULD YOU LIKE YOUR ENERGY LEVEL TO BE OVER THE NEXT 12 MONTHS?

1 · 2 · 3 · 4 · 5 · 6 · 7 · 8 · 9 · 10

Energy is a scarce resource. Many of the activities that we think will restore our energy don't. In fact, they drain energy while masquerading as relaxation. How often do people sit down to watch television, telling themselves they are going to relax for an hour, but end up falling asleep in front of the television? When was the last time you watched television for an hour or two, and then thought to yourself, "I'm all relaxed now, I feel like going to the gym to work out!" It doesn't happen.

It's time to start paying major attention to the people, places, things, and activities that energize you, and those that drain your energy.

NAME 3 PEOPLE THAT ENERGIZE YOU.

....

....

....

NAME 3 PEOPLE THAT DRAIN YOUR ENERGY.

....

....

....

NAME 3 PLACES THAT ENERGIZE YOU.

....

....

....

NAME 3 PLACES THAT DRAIN YOUR ENERGY.

....

....

....

NAME 3 THINGS THAT ENERGIZE YOU.

....

....

....

NAME 3 THINGS THAT DRAIN YOUR ENERGY.

....

....

....

NAME 3 ACTIVITIES THAT ENERGIZE YOU.

....

....

....

NAME 3 ACTIVITIES THAT DRAIN YOUR ENERGY.

....

....

....

How old would you be
if you didn't know how old you are?

SATCHEL PAIGE

26.

The Power of the Spoken Word

Words have power. Words spoken have power. Words unspoken have power.

Your words can encourage or discourage. They can inspire or depress. They can coach or criticize. They propagate love or hatred. They produce happiness or sadness. They can liberate others or enslave others.

EXERCISE #1: REFLECT FOR FIFTEEN MINUTES ON WORDS YOU WISH OTHER PEOPLE HAD SPOKEN TO YOU AT DIFFERENT TIMES THROUGHOUT YOUR LIFE.

Perhaps there was someone you needed to hear say, "I love you" or "I forgive you" or "You can do it" or "I'm sorry" or "I'm proud of you" or "Thank you." Whatever words you needed to hear at different times in your life from different people, jot them down.

WORDS YOU NEEDED TO HEAR / WHO YOU NEEDED TO HEAR THEM FROM

EXERCISE #2: REFLECT FOR FIFTEEN MINUTES ON SPECIFIC PEOPLE WHO COULD BENEFIT FROM HEARING CERTAIN WORDS FROM YOU.

Who are those people and what words are you being called to speak?

WORDS YOU NEED TO SPEAK / THE PERSON WHO NEEDS TO HEAR THEM

The ability to speak is an extraordinary gift, so is the ability to think. My father used to have these quips he would repeat to my brothers and me. "Engage brain before opening mouth," was one of them. It was a great lesson. It is a lesson I still need to be reminded of regularly, and one I now find myself sharing with my children.

So, let's take a few minutes and examine how we use the amazing gift of speech.

What percentage of your speech would be classified as positive or negative?

Do you speak your love?

Do you speak words of encouragement and affirmation?

Are you overly critical in your speech?

Do you praise yourself boastfully when speaking?

How often do you use words of anger?

Do you speak before considering what you are going to say?

When was the last time your words hurt someone?

Do you allow your mood to impact the way you speak to people?

Do you use profanity and obscenities when speaking?

How often do you use speech to complain?

How often do you engage in gossip?

Do you use negative humor to belittle others?

Are you dishonest in your speech?

Do you speak with kindness and courtesy to those you know and strangers?

Are you often argumentative with your speech?

Do you go out of your way to tell people they are doing simple things fabulously well?

Do you have the courage to use your speech to challenge other people when that is what you are called to do?

Saint Paul believed that just by guarding the way we speak and using the gift of speech deliberately, we could forge a path toward perfect unity with God. Every day we use our words to accomplish so many purposes, some of those purposes are admirable and some are not.

The gift of speech is an invitation to speak into the lives of the people who cross our paths. May our words be led by the Spirit and filled with goodness.

Old age is like everything else:
To make a success of it,
you've got to start young.

FRED ASTAIRE

27.
Your Most Important Relationships

Every person's life is an amazing adventure. We each have incredibly unique stories. But no matter where life takes us, when we come to the end of life, what matters most is remarkably similar for everyone: love, relationships, people.

WHICH DO YOU WANT TO BE SURROUNDED BY AT THE END, PEOPLE OR POSSESSIONS? And what type of people? Strangers or the people you share your rich and beautiful memories with?

The greatest joys in our lives are born from relationships. And our significant regrets are the result of relationship failures.

MAKE A LIST OF YOUR MOST IMPORTANT RELATIONSHIPS.
Take a few moments to reflect on each one. Pray for each
person. Then dream a little about how you would like each
relationship to grow and develop in your fourth quarter.

MY MOST IMPORTANT RELATIONSHIPS...

HERE ARE SEVEN WAYS TO IMPROVE YOUR RELATIONSHIPS IN YOUR FOURTH QUARTER:

1. Become a world class listener
2. Speak words of affirmation
3. Create experiences
4. Make acts of service a priority
5. Filter what you say with love, respect, humility, and discipline
6. Make an effort to be vulnerable
7. Ask people about their hopes and dreams

Life can only be understood backwards;
but it must be lived forwards.

SOREN KIERKEGAARD

28.

Say the Most Important Things

Communication is at the heart of any relationship. Most of us are not as good at communicating as we think we are. This is especially true when it comes to communicating our deepest thoughts and emotions. The biggest mistake we make in communication is thinking that saying something once is enough.

When asked by a therapist why he didn't tell his wife he loved her more often a man joked, "I told her I loved her when we got married. If anything changes, I will let her know."

What thoughts and feelings do you have when you read that? How do you perceive or judge that man?

It is often said, "Say what needs to be said before it's too late." But what is it that you need to say? And what is the most important thing to say?

Most people think the most important thing to say is "I love you." But long after people have passed from this world into the next, those of us who are left behind don't tend to obsess over whether or not someone loved us.

What do we obsess over? Two other matters of the heart.

The first surrounds forgiveness and unforgiveness. Many people are left wondering if their loved ones forgave them for something they did or said long ago. Others are left hurting because someone they loved never apologized for hurting them.

So, "I'm sorry" and "I forgive you" are high on the list of the most important things to say in the fourth quarter.

The cost of unforgiveness is multigenerational. Do whatever you can to remove this from your heart, your life, and your family line. Forgive and forgive often. "Bitter and resentful is no way to live. And it's definitely, no way to die." – *No Regrets*

One of the primary reasons that forgiveness is so critically important towards the end is because without forgiveness it is difficult for people to accept your love. If people don't believe that you have forgiven them, it is difficult for them to believe that you loved them.

The other matter our hearts get fixated on, especially with the loss of our parents, leaves children wondering if their parents were proud of them. When your parents died, were they proud of the person you had become and the way you were living your life? Very few people can answer this question with great confidence.

Give your children this gift. You may not agree with everything they do, but if you are proud of who they are becoming and the life they are living, tell them. Five words. "I am proud of you."

Let there be no uncertainty. If someone asks your children in the future, "Was your father proud of you?" "Was your mother proud of you?" give them the gift of knowing the answer to that question with great confidence.

It's important to say, "I love you." But it may be more important to say, "I'm sorry," "I forgive you," and "I am proud of you."

We cannot change the cards we are dealt, just how we play the hand.

RANDY PAUSCH

WHO ARE THE PEOPLE YOU WANT TO KNOW WITH ABSOLUTE CERTAINTY THAT YOU LOVED THEM WHEN YOU ARE GONE?

WHO ARE THE PEOPLE YOU NEED TO SAY "I'M SORRY" TO?

....

....

....

....

....

WHO ARE THE PEOPLE YOU NEED TO SAY "I FORGIVE YOU" TO?

....

....

....

....

....

IF YOU HAD TIME TO SAY JUST ONE THING, WHAT WOULD IT BE?

- I love you.
- I forgive you.
- I'm sorry.
- I'm so very proud of you.

If there is one thing I've learned
in my years on this planet,
it's that the happiest
and most fulfilled people
are those who devoted themselves
to something bigger
and more profound
than merely their own self-interest.

JOHN GLENN

29.

Your Fourth Quarter Talents

The fourth quarter is unique. It's a mistake to try to make the fourth quarter of life like the second quarter or third quarter. If you just do more of the same things you did during the second and third quarters of your life, you will miss out on what makes the fourth quarter unique. You may be called to do more of the same, but God calls us to activate very different talents and abilities in the fourth quarter.

God has given you so many talents. Some you may not even be aware of yet. This is the first truth about talents. God has given you so many talents that you cannot fully exercise even one of your talents in this lifetime. That's why it is essential that we turn to God from time to time and ask, "God, what talent do you want me to focus on now? Now that I am retired... or this year... or in this season of my life?"

There is a hidden talent within you that yearns to come alive in your fourth quarter more than ever before. Here's some examples:

Michael lived a very busy life obsessed with the affairs of business and career. Many people believed he was impatient and a horrible listener. After he retired, he let the ego associated with success and accomplishment relax, and he became incredibly patient and a fabulous listener. His children see him with his grandchildren and say, "He was never like that with me when I was a child." Michael doesn't disagree.

Stacy loved playing guitar as a teenager, but when she went to medical school, she set it in a corner and never went back to it. When she turned sixty, she picked it up again, and now plays every day. Once a week she makes a point to play for someone new. Sometimes she plays at parties and gatherings, and sometimes she visits retirement homes and plays for the residents.

Sofia wasn't able to have children. Her infertility was caused by a childhood disease. This was the source of tremendous heartache throughout her life. She didn't feel called to adopt but threw herself into serving others with her career. When she was sixty-one, her life changed forever with a single phone call, though she did not know it at the time. The call was from a friend who volunteered to watch a handful of young infants and toddlers while their mothers had their weekly book club. The other woman was sick and couldn't do it the next day. Sofia stepped in. Today Sofia is seventy-four and has not missed a single book club gathering in 13 years. "It has brought me a joy I cannot describe, a joy I never expected, a joy I never thought was possible," she explains.

Find your fourth quarter talent. We all have them. It's a matter of staying open.

The second truth about talents is that you have all the talents you need. You've got the perfect mix of talents necessary to live the life God created you to live. There is no point worrying about the talents you don't have. There is no point worrying about the talents your brothers, sisters, friends, parents, teachers, or anyone else has that you don't.

When it comes to talents, the ones you don't have, you don't need. If you needed them, God would have given them to you. God has given you the perfect mix of talents you need to live an amazing fourth quarter. This is just one of the many ways God provides for us.

You have talents that apply specifically to this stage of

life. They may have been dormant until now. Most people discover talents in their fourth quarter that they didn't even know they had. Your fourth quarter might reveal you as a great listener, it may be time to explore your creativity, or it may be time to develop spiritually. And most people rediscover a talent they discarded along the way.

WHAT HAVE BEEN THE DOMINANT TALENTS OF YOUR LIFE UP UNTIL NOW?

WHAT TALENTS IS GOD INVITING YOU TO EXPLORE IN YOUR FOURTH QUARTER?

....

....

....

....

....

You have exactly the gifts, talents, and abilities you need to live and thrive in the fourth quarter of your life.

To know how to grow old is the master work of wisdom, and one of the most difficult chapters in the great art of living.

HENRI FREDERIC AMIEL

30.

Give It Away

The attitude of giving or getting will define your fourth quarter. If you look at this season of life as a time to get, you will make yourself miserable. If you see this season as an opportunity to give more than ever before, you will experience the unmitigated joy you were created to taste in this life and be immersed in in the next life.

"The more you give yourself away, the happier you'll be." – *No Regrets*

When we think about giving we tend to think about being generous with money and things. We know people who are incredibly generous and we know others who are stingy. But most people think of themselves as generous.

Adopt the Generosity Habit. The Generosity Habit is simple: Give something away every day. It doesn't need to be money or material things. In fact, the philosophy behind the generosity habit rests on this singular truth: You don't need money or material possessions to live a life of staggering generosity.

The fourth quarter is a great time to intentionally adopt The Generosity Habit as a daily practice. It is a great time to unburden ourselves of surplus things. It is a perfect time to declutter our space so we can see clearly who we are and what we are being called to. But there is more.

One of the keys to living and dying with no regrets is clear, "Give yourself away." It is this self-donation, this gift of self, that matters most. Who or what have you laid down your life for until this point? Who or what is God calling you to gift yourself to in the fourth quarter?

It is the gift of self that matters most. Some parents have given their children the finest education money can buy, bought them cars and homes, and left them millions of dollars, but failed to give themselves to their children. And their children are left feeling empty and cheated.

Looking back over a lifetime, you see that love was the answer to everything.

RAY BRADBURY

LIST THREE TO FIVE PEOPLE YOU WANT TO POUR YOURSELF INTO IN YOUR FOURTH QUARTER.

....

....

....

....

....

Giving is one of the central themes of the fourth quarter. Become an expert in the matter. Leave behind a legacy of generosity.

Visit
TheGenerosityHabit.com
to watch
the FREE video series.

31.

Control and Surrender

If you want to make yourself and everyone around you miserable in your fourth quarter, try to control everything and everyone.

We spend so much of our lives trying to control situations, people, and things. These efforts are futile. Trying to be in control is a sure recipe for stress, anxiety, depression, and misery.

Sometimes people will say, "Let it go." I'm not going to say that. I realize that life is messy and there may be things you are not able to let go. So, what I will say to you is, let it be. It's hard to let things go, easier to let things be. What does it mean to let things be? It means to stop interfering, stop trying to control it, change it, or fix it. Just let it be.

The fourth quarter is the time to surrender to God if you haven't already. And if you have, it's time to renew that surrender.

You can wrestle with people and situations, with God

and time, but you will lose. And in the process, you will exhaust and frustrate yourself beyond belief.

Let me share four soul-shifting, life-changing words with you. If I could only give you four words to guide you through the fourth quarter, it would be these.

TRUST. SURRENDER. BELIEVE. RECEIVE.

EXERCISE: PRAY THESE FOUR WORDS ALOUD RIGHT NOW. TRUST. SURRENDER. BELIEVE. RECEIVE.

Repeat them slowly, over and over. Allow them to wash over you. Consider setting a timer for three minutes. Repeat these words slowly, thoughtfully, gently until the timer sounds.

TRUST. SURRENDER. BELIEVE. RECEIVE.

HOW DID REPEATING THOSE FOUR WORDS FOR THREE MINUTES MAKE YOU FEEL?

....

....

....

Pay attention to that. Ingrain that in your mind. Next time you are feeling stressed or anxious, take a minute or two, and just repeat those words over and over.

Once again we see the power of content in our lives. Those four words are content. What words or ideas (positive or negative) are you repeating to yourself in your heart and mind every day? How are those words and ideas impacting you?

The way of surrender is difficult. It requires renewed effort on a daily basis, often many times a day. We offer you this prayer of transformation as another tool to help you live into these four words.

It's not too late. It's important to remember that. God can accomplish in an afternoon what we cannot accomplish in a lifetime. He can do it in a single moment. It's not too late for God to transform you into the person He created you to be. It's not too late to unleash the goodness He has placed within you. It's not too late. Allow Him to work in you and your life.

The Prayer of Transformation

Loving Father,

Here I am.

I trust that you have an incredible plan for me.

Transform me. Transform my life.

Everything is on the table.

Take what you want to take and give what you want to give.

Transform me into the person you created me to be, so I can live the life you envision for me.

I hold nothing back;

I am 100 percent available.

How can I help?

Amen.

32.

Stay Open to Life

Do you sense yourself closing off to certain people and experiences as you get older? Are you less interested in activities? Have you lost interest in particular forms of entertainment? That's okay. There are some things we should close ourselves off to throughout our lives. This is necessary in order to separate the essential few from the trivial many so we can focus on what matters most.

The danger in the fourth quarter is to close ourselves off from everyone and everything. When we adopt this posture, we also close ourselves off from God, His plans, and His loving providence.

It is possible to focus on what matters most and stay open to new possibilities that God introduces.

Christians are people of possibility. This is true when we are children, and it remains true late in life.

Most people think of the fourth quarter as stale and

predictable. You are called to innovate in your fourth quarter as much as any other time in life. This innovation may have a different focus than at other times in your life. Your desired outcomes have probably shifted. But innovating how to simplify your life or innovating a new daily schedule can be fabulously life-giving.

Let me remind you of two words that have stimulated unfathomable hope and possibilities throughout history: What if... Men and women of every place and time have asked "What if..." and the results have been staggering in both ordinary and extraordinary ways.

What if... it's possible for man to walk on the moon.
What if... we can cure smallpox and polio.
What if... it's possible to run a mile in under four minutes.
What if... we can learn to forgive.
What if... we decide to go without wants, so others can have what they need.
What if... it's possible to experience God deeply and profoundly in this life.
What if... that relationship was able to be healed.
What if... it's possible to age gracefully and die peacefully.

What if... I can live a deeply satisfying life deep into my old age.

What if... I can go places, and do things, and meet new people.

What if... I treated every person I met for the rest of my life the way I would treat Jesus.

Don't let what you can't do interfere with what you can do. The fourth quarter is painted negatively by many, but it can be a time of positives and possibilities. Sometimes we need to test our assumptions. Often the things we believe are impossible are possible. It might be time to put together your own "What if..." list.

Aging is an extraordinary process where you become the person you always should have been.

DAVID BOWIE

MY "WHAT IF..." LIST

What if...

....

....

What if...

....

....

What if...

....

....

What if...

....

....

What if...

....

....

What if...

....

....

What if...

....

....

What if...

....

....

What if...

....

....

What if...

....

....

This list will open you to new positives and possibilities. Here is another fun question to ponder in specific situations. Think about something you would like to do or see happen, but you think is impossible or unlikely. Ask yourself: What would have to be true for X to happen?

Possibilities abound. There is plenty of negative to focus on if you choose. But there is plenty of positive. You get to choose. It's still a wonderful world filled with people who have an astounding capacity for goodness.

Stay open to life.

33.

Be a Great Encourager

When we think about the Father, Son, and Holy Spirit, we all have different images and experiences to draw on. I have come to believe that the Holy Spirit is the Great Encourager. And we all need encouragement.

We all have people in our lives who have encouraged us along the way. And we all have people in our lives who have criticized us along the way.

LIST THREE PEOPLE WHO HAVE BEEN A SOURCE OF ENCOURAGEMENT FOR YOU.

....

....

....

HOW DO YOU FEEL ABOUT THE PEOPLE WHO HAVE ENCOURAGED YOU?

....

....

....

LIST THREE PEOPLE WHO HAVE BEEN CRITICAL OF YOU.

....

....

....

HOW DO YOU FEEL ABOUT THE PEOPLE WHO HAVE BEEN CRITICAL OF YOU?

....

....

....

Thinking about the people who have been critical of you throughout your life may give rise to feelings of anger and resentment. It's important to acknowledge those feelings, but not to ruminate upon them.

The primary purpose of the exercise is to explore the impact other people's encouragement and criticism has had on you and your life. The obvious question this reflection leads us to is: Do you want to be a voice of encouragement or a voice of criticism in your fourth quarter?

You may have been a negative naysayer all your life up until now. That's unfortunate, but changeable. You can change. It's one of the most enthralling things about human beings. We can change.

Don't let yourself get stuck on the road of regret when you reflect on the past. Learn what you need to learn to thrive in the fourth quarter and keep moving. You cannot change one minute of the past, but you can influence every moment going forward. Don't let your past rob you of your future.

Do you want to be remembered as a critical voice or an encouraging voice?

We all need encouragement. That's why the Holy Spirit is constantly encouraging us to listen to the gentle voice within, to choose the path of character and integrity.

There is a lot of talk about legacy in our culture. As people transition from the first half of life to the second half of life, that conversation has been dominated by the idea of moving from success to significance. The conversation about legacy intensifies as people enter the fourth quarter, even if only in our minds. A legacy of encouragement is a fine legacy to leave behind and be remembered by.

Decide, here and now, today, to make encouragement one of the great themes of your fourth quarter.

NOW, TAKE A MOMENT TO NAME AND PRAY IN THANKSGIVING FOR THE PEOPLE WHO HAVE ENCOURAGED YOU THROUGHOUT YOUR LIFE.

....

....

....

....

....

10 PEOPLE YOU WANT TO ENCOURAGE. Who will you encourage? How often?

34.

Set Your Mind on the Things Above

There is a spectacular passage in Paul's letter to the Philippians that reads, "Finally, brothers and sisters, whatever is true, whatever is noble, whatever is right, whatever is pure, whatever is lovely, whatever is admirable—if anything is excellent or praiseworthy—think about such things (Philippians 4:8)."

What do you spend your days and weeks thinking about? Do you think about things that raise you up or pull you down? Things that energize you or drain your energy? Things that bring you joy or things that make you angry?

Truth, beauty, and goodness are the pillars of creation, wisdom, and a life well-lived. All three are under attack in today's culture, but even if the world would become a place where there is no place for truth, beauty, and goodness, there should always be a place for these things in our hearts and minds.

Human thought is incredibly powerful. Human thought is creative. Whatever we choose to focus our thoughts on tends to increase in our lives and in our character.

WHAT THREE TOPICS HAVE YOU SPENT THE MOST TIME THINKING ABOUT DURING YOUR LIFE SO FAR?

....

....

....

WHICH THREE TOPICS DO YOU WANT TO SPEND THE MOST TIME THINKING ABOUT DURING THE FOURTH QUARTER OF YOUR LIFE?

....

....

....

If you ask a group of people to list some of the exceptional abilities they have witnessed in other people throughout their lives, they will come up with a vast and varied list. The list may include things such as: Violinist. Teacher. Coach. Mother. Entrepreneur. Artist. Nurse. Doctor. Scientist. Baseball player. Author. Father. Friend. Leader. Mechanic. Chef.

Each of these can be exceptional in their own right, but even more exceptional, and of greater importance, are the hidden abilities that lay beneath them all. One example of such an ability is focus.

Our ability to focus (or not) can have enormous impact on the outcomes of our lives. In many ways, all you need to do to live an amazing fourth quarter is focus. Focus on what? That is what these exercises are all about, discovering what YOU should focus on.

But I am sure of this, whatever you choose to focus on in this season of your life will increase. If you focus on your regrets, you will multiply them. If you focus on the ways people have hurt you, you will become increasingly bitter and resentful. If you focus on "whatever is true, whatever is noble, whatever is right, whatever is pure, whatever is lovely, whatever is admirable—anything excellent or praiseworthy" these too will increase in your life.

What you choose to focus on can make all the difference. The fourth quarter is a time to focus and reflect. Give yourself time to think in this season of your life. Lots of time. Think deeply. Think broadly. Immerse yourself in truth, beauty, and goodness. There is nothing else in Heaven.

It stands to reason that anyone who
learns to live well will die well.
The skills are the same:
being present in the moment,
and humble,
and brave,
and keeping a sense of humor.

VICTORIA MORAN

35.

Don't Leave a Mess

Money and things are wonderful if they are used intentionally. But both have the ability to complicate our lives, distract us from what matters most, create discord and division in our families, and prevent us from growing spiritually.

A common and significant fourth quarter oversight is to leave a mess for those you leave behind to clean up. Such a mess can exacerbate the grieving process or can rob people of the chance to properly grieve and heal, because of the demands the worldly mess places upon them.

The mess in times past consisted primarily of closets, basements, and garages full of stuff. Those left behind are left to sift through all this stuff trying to work out what is of value, financially or otherwise, and what is not.

The next iteration of the practical and existential mess is the absence of clear direction for your heirs. Only forty-five percent of American adults have a Last Will and

Testament. When someone dies without one, this creates chaos and confusion for their loved ones.

And finally, in the modern world, the capacity for the mess extends far beyond money and things. Something as simple as missing passwords can make life very frustrating for a spouse or child who is left behind.

Here is a list of items to consider completing and organizing in one place for the people you love and will be leaving behind:

- Your Last Will and Testament
- Estate Plan
- Name and Contact Information of Executor
- Contact Information for Attorney and Accountant
- Deeds and Titles for all Assets
- Life Insurance Account Numbers and Contact Information
- Bank Account Numbers and Contact Information
- Retirement Accounts and Contact Information
- Credit Card Accounts and Contact Information
- List of Regular Bills, especially those on autopay
- List of Mileage Accounts and Other Loyalty/Reward Programs
- Comprehensive List of Passwords

Add to the list according to your own situation but make a firm resolution not to leave a mess. It can be very stressful for the people you leave behind. It can rob them of the chance to fully experience the grieving process. It can create a legacy of resentment.

Set your affairs in order. Simplify your material possessions. Liberate your garage, closet, and basement of anything that is not necessary to your life in the fourth quarter. These are real and practical ways to express love and care for those closest to you.

There is no secret to the good life.
It isn't a mystery.
What is the essential ingredient?
Goodness itself.
If you wish to live the good life,
fill your life with goodness.
Fill your life with love, kindness,
gratitude, compassion, and generosity.

LIFE IS MESSY

36.

Every Family Needs a Prayerful Giant

Every family needs a prayerful giant. What is a prayerful giant? A prayerful giant is someone who dedicates him or herself to praying for their family—past, present, and future generations.

Prayerlessness is one of the great torments of modern times. For decades the time we spend in focused prayer has been diminishing as our lives have become busier. We have fallen into the tyranny of the urgent, which demands that we rush from one urgent thing to the next. The problem with this is that the most important things are hardly ever urgent. This can leave us always doing urgent things but never doing important things. It is the most important things that we never get around to in this cycle. Prayer is one of those important things. It is particularly important because prayer helps us to identify what matters most and strengthens our hearts to give priority to those things in our daily lives. What could be more important than prayer?

Prayerlessness distorts the human person. Without prayer, over time we forget the attitudes and qualities that make us uniquely human (compassion, generosity, humility, empathy, fortitude) and we become more and more like mere animals.

Prayer leads us to catch a glimpse of the-best-version-of-ourselves and helps us to develop the virtue necessary to celebrate our best selves. If you watch your evening news tonight you will discover that the world desperately needs men and women of prayer and virtue. People in your neighborhood need your prayers, your church needs your prayers, your colleagues at work need your prayers, and your family needs you to become a prayerful giant.

Over the years, I have encountered many great families in my travels. A number of years ago I started trying to work out what made these families so steadfast and full of life. Tolstoy begins the epic novel *Anna Karenina* with these lines: "Happy families are all alike; every unhappy family is unhappy in its own way." What I have discovered is that all the great families I have encountered have a giant of prayer. These prayerful giants pray constantly for their families, surrounding them with God's grace and protection.

Somewhere in the not-too-distant past of these families is a person who was a prayerful giant.

A prayerful giant is a person who covers their family with prayer, anchoring the family in God's grace. Sometimes it is the grandmother or grandfather, the mother or father, an uncle or aunt, and from time to time you have to go back two or three generations, sometimes more to find the family's prayerful giant. But you always find a prayerful giant in their family tree. Every family needs a cornerstone of prayer to pray for the family, now and in the future.

LIST 5 QUALITIES OR VALUES YOU WOULD LIKE YOUR FAMILY TO EMBRACE FOR THE NEXT THOUSAND YEARS AND BEYOND.

....

....

....

....

....

LIST THE PEOPLE IN YOUR FAMILY FROM PAST, PRESENT, AND FUTURE GENERATIONS THAT YOU WOULD LIKE TO PRAY FOR IN YOUR FOURTH QUARTER.

I suppose if a family gets far enough down the road from that prayerful giant without raising up another, its members begin to lose their way. Does it take a generation or two? Does it take three or four? I don't know. I suppose it depends on many variables. But in each generation, each family needs at least one of these men and women of faithful prayer to guide and protect it.

Your family needs a prayerful giant. Commit your fourth quarter to becoming a man or woman of prayer. Let part of your legacy be a legacy of prayer.

What we need most
in order to make progress
is to be silent before this great God,
for the language he best hears
is silent love.

SAINT JOHN OF THE CROSS

37.
Three Appointments

We are all required to keep three appointments in life. The appointment with self, the appointment with God, and the inevitable appointment with death. We may avoid, deny, resist, ignore, and otherwise pretend that these appointments are not on our schedule. It matters not. Life brings about these appointments whether we think we are ready or not.

The first appointment is with self. It's amazing how we avoid ourselves. Few things contribute more to our collective sense that something is missing and that we are living someone else's life than the avoidance of self.

Long ago, I learned to keep a daily appointment with self. Unless I check in with myself each day, I will eventually betray myself in small ways and large. But when I keep this appointment, I emerge with a clear and firm sense of self. This sense of self—knowing who we are and what we are here for—is more precious than gold.

The quality of all our relationships is determined by the quality of our relationship with ourselves. This is one of the many reasons the first appointment is critical. When we avoid this appointment, we limit all of our relationships.

The second appointment is with God. We avoid God, run from him, thinking that we want something other than what He wants to give us. But in running from God, we run from ourselves. Alienation from God is alienation from self. Only in union with God do we discover and become our truest self.

When we discover how messy and difficult life is, we hear an urgent call to remake and rebuild the inner life. What was once an invitation quickly turns into a summons. Not the summons of a tyrannical God that demands we pay attention, but rather, the summons of our own soul to pay attention before it wilts and dies.

Turn to God each day for some period of time. Who else will lead you to green pastures and peaceful waters? Who else will make your cup overflow? Who else will restore your soul?

I don't know about you, but I need that. My soul needs to be restored.

The third appointment is with death. It is the inescapable

truth. It is a non-negotiable assignment. In one of his movies, Jack Nicholson is walking through a bar when he recognizes someone he knows. He doesn't stop, but he slows down. "How are you?" he asks. The guy begins to complain about something and Jack cuts him off, "We're all dying. Act accordingly." Is it blunt? Yes. Is it true? Yes. We are all dying, but we don't act accordingly.

"Every man dies, but not every man really lives," was William Wallace's observation. Nobody fears death more than those who have not lived. Nobody fears death more than those who have not discovered who they are and offered that gift to the world. Death is inevitable, but a well-lived life is not.

When you come to the end of your life, when death is undeniably near, what will bring you unmitigated joy? Thinking about death is morbid some may say. I disagree. Far from being unhealthy, it is a valuable and meaningful exercise. Thinking too much about death can be morbid, but how much is too much? I suggest that you think about death only as much as is necessary to live life to the fullest.

When we are young it feels like we have all the time in the world. But we don't. Sooner than we expect, we begin to slow down. We can't do the things we used to be able to do. All the time our bodies are breaking down, though we often don't acknowledge it until we get sick or are dying. How will you feel when you are dying? What will you think? It is an appointment we all must keep. Don't arrive unprepared.

If you found out today that you were dying, what would be your regrets? What do those regrets tell you about how you are living your life? What changes do those regrets invite you to make?

The wisest people of every age have pondered death and eternity. Not as an exercise in morbidity, but in order to live life to the fullest.

Death and the knowledge of its inevitability serve an important purpose in our lives. Imagine how carelessly and recklessly people would live if they knew they would live forever in this world.

If living a meaningful life depends on filling our lives with meaningful activity, these three appointments should figure regularly on our schedule. These three appointments help us to weed out the meaningless from the meaningful. They help us prioritize what matters most and give us the courage to say no to what matters least. They build within us a true sense of self, and few things are more important. These three appointments, in short, keep us alert and aware of our blessings, help us to become more perfectly ourselves, and live life to the fullest.

WHICH OF THESE APPOINTMENTS DO YOU MOST NEED TO ATTEND TO?

....

....

While you are alive,
feel and know that you are alive.
When you are feeling sorry for yourself
about what you used to be able to do,
do something new.

MOTHER TERESA

WRITE DOWN ONE WAY YOU CAN MORE FULLY EMBRACE EACH OF THE THREE APPOINTMENTS.

Appointment with Self:

Appointment with God:

Appointment with Death:

38.

Life After Death

What do you think happens when we die?

Where do you think we go?

What do you think we experience?

These are questions that people have been asking for thousands of years. Nobody knows the answer to these questions entirely, but that doesn't mean we should stop pondering them.

Do you think much about Heaven?

Are you curious about Heaven?

Are you curious about God?

Are you curious about the afterlife?

We should be. We should be a lot more curious about these things than we are. If you are going on vacation, think about all the things you want to know before you go. If you were moving to a new home in a new city, think of all the things you would be curious about. We should be more curious about how, where, and with whom we are going to spend eternity.

Another question worth considering that we tend to avoid is: How do you want to die?

Have you ever thought about it? Some people think it's morbid to think about their death, but not thinking about it doesn't improve the experience, and tends to increase the stress and anxiety people have around dying.

Do you want to be angry, bitter, twisted, and resentful when you die? Most people know the answer to this question is clearly no, but there are many people who die this way.

The great Christian thinkers for over a thousand years have encouraged people to meditate on the Four Last Things: Death, Judgement, Heaven, and Hell.

Some may say this is old fashioned. Others will have new excuses to ignore these meditations. But reflecting on these four realities helps us to live more intentionally and to age gracefully and die peacefully.

The Four Last Things are not intended to frighten us, but rather to help us live and die more beautifully. Have you lived a beautiful life? Maybe you have, maybe you haven't. What matters most now is what you do next. Start living a beautiful life today. One day at a time. Make today a beautiful day.

Most of all, reflecting on the Last Four Things makes the necessity of a spiritual life abundantly clear. The fourth quarter is a time to develop a robust spiritual life. If you don't know where to start, that's okay. Seek out the people and resources that can help you develop a dynamic spiritual life.

When the final days, weeks, months, and hours of life approach, few things will comfort you like your connection with God.

WRITE A BRIEF DESCRIPTION OF HOW YOU WOULD LIKE TO DIE. Let your imagination take over. Where? When? State of mind? State of soul? Who would you like to be there?

39.

Read the Book

Many years ago, when I was travelling from city to city, night after night, I used to share a humorous rendition of arriving at the gates of Heaven.

"How are you?" God would ask you.

"I'm good, God. Well, I mean, I think I'm good. I mean, I'm dead. So, maybe I should ask you, how am I God?" you would reply.

"Let's not get bogged down with those details right now," God would say. "But let me ask you something. Did you read my book?"

Now that's an awkward moment. We have all had some awkward moments in our lives, but when God asks if you read His book, that has the potential to be a genuine, certified, awkward moment.

"Sort of," you reply sheepishly.

"What do you mean, sort of?" God asks looking for details.

"Well, I read bits and pieces," you reply.

"Bits and pieces? What do you mean bits and pieces?" God asks.

"Well, God, you know, at church on Sunday, they always read some bits and pieces, and I tried to listen," you explain.

And now God looks a little disappointed. And justifiably, I think. I mean, He's only got the one book. It's not like He is John Grisham with a new book every two weeks.

The people would laugh, but it was a laughter laced with anxiety. For something about the story struck a nerve of truth and knowing.

The story was designed to get people laughing, but it was also designed to illustrate the insanity of passing through this world without reading God's book.

Wherever you are in your life, start reading the Bible for a few minutes each day. Where should you start? Start with the New Testament. Read one chapter a day. From that one chapter, pick a word, phrase, or idea that strikes you, and talk to God about it.

One chapter a day. When you are done with the New Testament, begin with the Old Testament. You don't need to become a Biblical Scholar. Just allow God to speak into the rest of your life through His Word.

Most people overestimate what they can do in a day, and underestimate what they can do in a month.
We overestimate what we can do in a year, and underestimate what we can accomplish in a decade.

THE LONG VIEW

40.

Begin Each Day This Way

How do you begin each day? What are your morning routines and rituals? How do your days unfold differently if you skip steps in your morning routines?

WRITE DOWN YOUR MORNING ROUTINES. Include the positive and the negative habits that have become a part of each morning.

....

....

....

....

....

WHICH THREE MORNING ROUTINES OR RITUALS ARE SERVING YOU BEST?

....

....

....

WHICH MORNING HABITS DO YOU FEEL CALLED TO STOP DOING?

....

....

....

Og Mandino, the American speaker, author, motivator, and philosopher, was legendary for helping people see possibilities. Many years ago, a friend shared one of his more famous lines with me, and it has stuck with me ever since.

"I will greet each day with love in my heart." This was Mandino's counsel.

What was in your heart this morning as you greeted today?

It's an interesting concept. Most people get out of bed and wait to see what happens. But greeting each day with love in your heart requires intentionality. And let me say, it is harder than you think. There will be days when you don't feel inclined to greet the day with love in your heart.

Routines and rituals, large and small, personal and communal, are critically important in the fourth quarter. What will your daily rituals be? What will your morning routines be? You may want to adopt Og's suggestion: "Greet each day with love in my heart."

Conclusion: Embracing What Matters Most

I had an experience in the Scouts as a teen that provides an interesting metaphor for modern life. One Friday night, we went to every fast-food restaurant within ten miles. The idea was to have a little of something at each place. But we were young and excited and foolish.

Our first stop was at Homestead Chicken. Their fried chicken was exquisite, but they also had these seasoned fries that were nothing short of addictive. By the time we left our first stop of what was going to be a long night, most of us had already eaten enough for the weekend. But we pressed on, hour after hour, stop after stop, eating more and more, ignoring all signs that with each extra bite we experienced less satisfaction and more discomfort.

At the end of this fast-food crawl, we had all eaten so much we felt sick. Unable to control ourselves, we had sacrificed satisfaction for gluttony. We were full but we were empty.

In a culture of unlimited options, it is easy to move from one thing to the next, gluttonously indulging, never pausing long enough to ask life's bigger questions. Too many people live and die that way: dissatisfied.

It's time to discern and embrace what matters most. It is our hope that this book has helped you to do that as you prepare for the fourth quarter of your life.

What matters most? It is one of those deceptively simple questions that opens layer upon layer in our hearts, minds, and souls.

The world throws a million things at us, so we approach life as a taste-testing experience at an all you can eat buffet. But satisfaction is born by committing ourselves to the few people, things, and experiences that matter most. Wisdom is discerning the vital few and pouring ourselves into them. Wisdom chooses the vital few over the trivial many, and in some matters, the one over all others.

What matters most? Hold this question before you for a few minutes each day. Allow the wisdom of the vital few to emerge, so that you can reject the trivial many and embrace what matters most.

What matters most... people or things?

What matters most... yesterday or
today?

What matters most... accomplishments or
friendships?

What matters most... the school you went to or
what you learned?

What matters most... the house you live in or
the love in your home?

What matters most... the things you collect or
the person you become?

What matters most... the way people perceive you or
who you are?

What matters most... age or
attitude?

What matters most... how much money you have or
how you spend your money?

What matters most... what you say or
what you do?

What matters most... how long you live or
what you do with the years God gives you?

What matters most... who is right or
what is right?

What matters most... the body or
the soul?

What matters most... this world or
the next?

What matters most... that we were successful or
that we loved?

What matters most... doing things right or
doing the right things?

What matters most... getting or
giving?

What matters most... what we have lost or
what we have found?

What matters most... the lines on our faces or
the experiences that made them?

It's the fourth quarter. It's time to be brutally honest with ourselves. No matter where we have been, what we have done, how we have succeeded or failed, it is time to be honest with ourselves about what matters most. It's time to place who and what matters most at the center of our lives and let all the selfishness and triviality slip away.

The fourth quarter of life can be an amazing time. But it will not simply happen. It requires intentionality and vigilance. Knowing what matters most will allow you to make this season of your life a rich and rewarding experience for yourself and for those you love.